Library / Media Center
Carroll
1601
W9-ADI-706
Westminster, Maryland 21157

1 JEFFERSON MEMORIAL
14th Street and E. Basin
Drive, SW

2 UNITED STATES HOLOCAUST
MEMORIAL MUSEUM
100 Raoul Wallenberg Place
(between D Street and
Independence Avenue, SW)

3 DEPARTMENT OF AGRICULTURE
14th Street and Independence
Avenue, SW

LIBRARY OF CONGRESS:

4 THOMAS JEFFERSON BUILDING
1st Street and Independence
Avenue, SE

5 JOHN ADAMS BUILDING
2nd Street and Independence
Avenue, SE

6 JAMES MADISON MEMORIAL
BUILDING
101 Independence Avenue, SE

7 FOLGER SHAKESPEARE LIBRARY
201 E. Capitol Street, SE

8 MARY MCLEOD BETHUNE
MEMORIAL
Lincoln Park, E. Capitol and
12th Streets, NE

9 SUPREME COURT OF THE
UNITED STATES
1st Street, NE (between Maryland
Avenue and E. Capitol Street)

10 UNITED STATES CAPITOL
Entrance at E. Capitol Street on
Capitol Hill

11 ROBERT A. TAFT MEMORIAL
Capitol Grounds (between
Constitution, New Jersey, and
Louisiana Avenues, NW)

12 UNION STATION
Massachusetts Avenue, NE
(between 1st and 2nd Streets)

13 NATIONAL POSTAL MUSEUM
Massachusetts Avenue, NE
(between N. Capitol and 1st
Streets)

14 NATIONAL ARCHIVES
Constitution Avenue and 8th
Street, NW

15 DEPARTMENT OF JUSTICE
9th Street and Constitution
Avenue, NW

16 FORMER POST OFFICE
DEPARTMENT BUILDING
12th Street and Pennsylvania
Avenue, NW

17 FREEDOM PLAZA
Pennsylvania Avenue, NW
(between 13th and 14th Streets)

18 DEPARTMENT OF COMMERCE
14th Street, NW (between E
Street and Constitution Avenue)

19 NATIONAL MUSEUM
OF AMERICAN HISTORY
Constitution Avenue and 14th
Street, NW

20 CONSTITUTION HALL
18th and D Streets, NW

21 VIETNAM VETERANS MEMORIAL
21st Street and Constitution
Avenue, NW

22 LINCOLN MEMORIAL
23rd Street, NW (west end of
Mall)

23 JOHN F. KENNEDY CENTER
FOR THE PERFORMING ARTS
New Hampshire Avenue, NW,
and Rock Creek Parkway

24 THEODORE ROOSEVELT
MEMORIAL
Roosevelt Island, Potomac River
(adjacent to the George
Washington Memorial Parkway
and Key Bridge)

ARLINGTON NATIONAL
CEMETERY:

25 TOMB OF THE UNKNOWNS
off Memorial Drive

26 ARLINGTON MEMORIAL
AMPHITHEATER
off Memorial Drive

27 JOHN F. KENNEDY AND ROBERT
F. KENNEDY GRAVESITES
off Sheridan Drive, Arlington
National Cemetery

WITHDRAWN

INSCRIPTIONS OF A NATION

Collected Quotations from
Washington Monuments

ↄ

Clint W. Ensign

CONGRESSIONAL QUARTERLY

Washington, D.C.

To Cindy and our children

❧

Cover photograph: Detail from Columbus Fountain, Union Station

Copyright © 1994 by Congressional Quarterly Inc.
1414 22nd Street, N.W., Washington, D.C. 20037

All rights reserved. No part of this publication may be reproduced or transmitted in any form
or by any means, electronic or mechanical, including photocopy, recording, or any information storage
and retrieval system, without permission in writing from the publisher.

Produced by Elliott & Clark Publishing, Washington, D.C.
Designed by Gibson Parsons Design
Edited by Elizabeth Brown Lockman
Illustrations © 1994 by J. Michael Osteen. All rights reserved.
Cover photograph © 1994 by Robert Llewellyn. All rights reserved.

Printed in the United States of America

Library of Congress Cataloging-in-Publication Data

Ensign, Clint W.
Inscriptions of a Nation / Clint W. Ensign.
p.   cm.
Includes index.
ISBN 0-87187-962-X
1. Architectural inscriptions—Washington (D.C.) 2. Washington
(D.C.)—Public buildings. 3. Quotations. I. Title.
NA4050. I5E57 1994
729' .19' 09753—dc20   94-23104
                                                                         CIP

CONTENTS

PREFACE

*S*everal years ago, I was surprised to learn that there was no book that contained the inscriptions from the major memorials, historic buildings, and structures in the nation's capital. And so began my efforts to prepare *Inscriptions of a Nation*. In doing so, my intent has been to make accessible a comprehensive collection of these writings that have both national and universal application. The process has been enjoyable, largely because of the penetrating meaning and worth of this literature.

Cut in stone or otherwise permanently written on walls for public viewing, these quotations were carefully selected for their enduring inspirational value. Representing a rich literary and historic archive, the writings cover a wide diversity of subjects: government and freedom, war and suffering, education and commerce, justice and history, literature and the arts. When combined, the writings embody the essence of American character, feelings, and ideals.

The principal focus of the book is the inscriptions themselves. Although these writings originate from a variety of sources, and many accompany sculptural or architectural decorations, I felt that a detailed explanation of each quotation and its setting would detract from this primary focus. However, to provide background, a brief historical essay introduces each section.

In some instances, the inscriptions recorded in this book vary slightly from those at the actual site. Most of these differences relate to punctuation marks. In making the book more readable, I have followed written texts whenever they were available and have tried to present the material in the most accurate light.

With the exception of the major memorials or buildings, I have excluded dedicatory building inscriptions. Quotations from scores of military monuments and sites are likewise excluded. I also did not include inscriptions that can only be understood by seeing the paintings or sculptures they accompany.

The quotations cited in this book are from commonly visited public sites. While the White House meets this criterion, access to the building is far more restricted than it is at most other sites. Because of this, and because the White House contains only one inscription, a separate section on this structure is not included. However, as a matter of reference, the following inscription from the writings of John Adams is found in the fireplace mantel of the State Dining Room: "I pray Heaven to Bestow the Best of Blessings on THIS HOUSE and All that shall hereafter Inhabit it. May none but Honest and Wise Men ever rule under this Roof."

Of note is that no inscriptions were found at the Washington Monument. Also, the names of the more than 58,000 men and women on the Wall at the Vietnam Veterans Memorial are not included in this book.

I was significantly aided in my research by staff at the Department of the Interior, the United States Holocaust Memorial Museum, the John F. Kennedy Center for the Performing Arts, the Daughters of the American Revolution, the Architect of the Capitol, the Smithsonian Institution, the Folger Shakespeare Library, the U. S. Postal Service, the Department of Justice, the Department of Agriculture, the Pennsylvania Avenue Development Corporation, the Library of Congress, and Bethune-Cookman College. If there are mistakes, omissions, or errors within these pages, they are completely unintended and solely my responsibility.

I extend special thanks to Lois Whetzel, who reviewed my initial version of *Inscriptions of a Nation* and offered many helpful suggestions. I also thank Renae Hillyard, who spent personal time assisting with technical details of the book. And most of all, I extend my sincere appreciation to my wife Cindy for her constant support and patience with this effort. From the beginning, she firmly believed in the value of this work and was a tremendous source of encouragement and assistance.

—*Clint W. Ensign, June 1994*

JEFFERSON MEMORIAL

A brilliant individual and statesman, Thomas Jefferson was a central figure in the American Revolution and in the development of the new nation. He was also the sole architect in drafting the Declaration of Independence.

Jefferson was a devoted and skilled public servant who held a variety of state and national offices, including that of United States president. One exceptional accomplishment of Jefferson was the Louisiana Purchase, which greatly expanded the United States' borders and enhanced its security. He was raised in Virginia's southern frontier, which strongly influenced his love for country life. His Virginia estate Monticello demonstrates the depth of his intellect and ingenuity in the sciences, horticulture, and architecture.

In 1772, Jefferson married Martha Wayles Skelton. A decade later she died, and Jefferson was never to remarry during the remaining 44 years of his life. He died at Monticello on July 4, 1826, exactly one-half century after the Declaration of Independence was signed.

Inscriptions at the memorial were selected by the Thomas Jefferson Memorial Commission and were taken from a wide variety of his writings on freedom, slavery, education, and government. The memorial was dedicated in 1943 and was designed by John Russell Pope. The 19-foot bronze statue of Jefferson is the work of Rudulph Evans.

I HAVE SWORN UPON THE ALTAR OF GOD ETERNAL HOSTILITY
AGAINST EVERY FORM OF TYRANNY OVER THE MIND OF MAN.

WE HOLD THESE TRUTHS TO BE SELF-EVIDENT: THAT ALL MEN ARE
CREATED EQUAL, THAT THEY ARE ENDOWED BY THEIR CREATOR WITH
CERTAIN INALIENABLE RIGHTS, AMONG THESE ARE LIFE, LIBERTY, AND
THE PURSUIT OF HAPPINESS, THAT TO SECURE THESE RIGHTS GOVERN-
MENTS ARE INSTITUTED AMONG MEN. WE ... SOLEMNLY PUBLISH AND
DECLARE, THAT THESE COLONIES ARE AND OF RIGHT OUGHT TO BE FREE
AND INDEPENDENT STATES.... AND FOR THE SUPPORT OF THIS DECLA-
RATION, WITH A FIRM RELIANCE ON THE PROTECTION OF DIVINE PROVI-
DENCE, WE MUTUALLY PLEDGE OUR LIVES, OUR FORTUNES, AND OUR
SACRED HONOUR.

ALMIGHTY GOD HATH CREATED THE MIND FREE. ALL ATTEMPTS TO INFLUENCE IT BY TEMPORAL PUNISHMENTS OR BURTHENS ... ARE A DEPARTURE FROM THE PLAN OF THE HOLY AUTHOR OF OUR RELIGION.... NO MAN SHALL BE COMPELLED TO FREQUENT OR SUPPORT ANY RELIGIOUS WORSHIP OR MINISTRY OR SHALL OTHERWISE SUFFER ON ACCOUNT OF HIS RELIGIOUS OPINIONS OR BELIEF, BUT ALL MEN SHALL BE FREE TO PROFESS AND BY ARGUMENT TO MAINTAIN THEIR OPINIONS IN MATTERS OF RELIGION. I KNOW BUT ONE CODE OF MORALITY FOR MEN WHETHER ACTING SINGLY OR COLLECTIVELY.

❧

GOD WHO GAVE US LIFE GAVE US LIBERTY. CAN THE LIBERTIES OF A NATION BE SECURE WHEN WE HAVE REMOVED A CONVICTION THAT THESE LIBERTIES ARE THE GIFT OF GOD? INDEED I TREMBLE FOR MY COUNTRY WHEN I REFLECT THAT GOD IS JUST, THAT HIS JUSTICE CANNOT SLEEP FOREVER. COMMERCE BETWEEN MASTER AND SLAVE IS DESPOTISM. NOTHING IS MORE CERTAINLY WRITTEN IN THE BOOK OF FATE THAN THAT THESE PEOPLE ARE TO BE FREE. ESTABLISH THE LAW FOR EDUCATING THE COMMON PEOPLE. THIS IT IS THE BUSINESS OF THE STATE TO EFFECT AND ON A GENERAL PLAN.

I AM NOT AN ADVOCATE FOR FREQUENT CHANGES IN LAWS AND CON-
STITUTIONS, BUT LAWS AND INSTITUTIONS MUST GO HAND IN HAND
WITH THE PROGRESS OF THE HUMAN MIND. AS THAT BECOMES MORE
DEVELOPED, MORE ENLIGHTENED, AS NEW DISCOVERIES ARE MADE,
NEW TRUTHS DISCOVERED AND MANNERS AND OPINIONS CHANGE,
WITH THE CHANGE OF CIRCUMSTANCES, INSTITUTIONS MUST ADVANCE
ALSO TO KEEP PACE WITH THE TIMES. WE MIGHT AS WELL REQUIRE A
MAN TO WEAR STILL THE COAT WHICH FITTED HIM WHEN A BOY AS
CIVILIZED SOCIETY TO REMAIN EVER UNDER THE REGIMEN OF THEIR
BARBAROUS ANCESTORS.

UNITED STATES HOLOCAUST
MEMORIAL MUSEUM

*T*he inscription "For The Dead And The Living We Must Bear Witness" marks the entrance to the Hall of Remembrance of the United States Holocaust Memorial Museum. The museum tells the overpowering story of the systematic genocide of millions of Jews and other Europeans at the hands of Nazi Germany from 1933 to 1945. The Hall of Remembrance is the national memorial to the Holocaust victims. The Permanent Exhibition of the museum is found on three separate floors and covers three historic periods: the Nazi Assault (1933-1939), the Final Solution (1940-1944), and the Aftermath (1945-present). The Children's Wall of Remembrance is a memorial to the estimated 1.5 million children who died in the Holocaust. Educational centers, auditoriums, special exhibition galleries, and the Library and Archives are also part of the museum. The Eisenhower Plaza on the building's western side is dedicated to General Dwight D. Eisenhower and the Allied soldiers who liberated the Holocaust survivors.

The design for the museum was developed by James I. Freed of New York, in

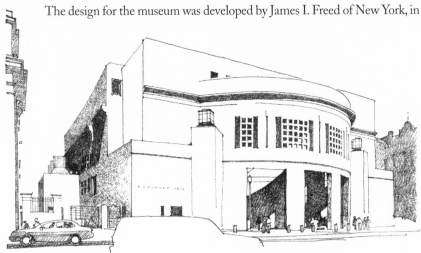

association with Notter, Finegold, and Alexander, Inc. of Washington, D.C. The memorial was dedicated in 1993. Adjacent to the National Mall, it is located 400 yards south of the Washington Monument. Inscriptions are found on both its exterior and interior.

Exterior

OUT OF OUR MEMORY ... OF THE HOLOCAUST WE MUST FORGE AN UNSHAKABLE OATH WITH ALL CIVILIZED PEOPLE THAT NEVER AGAIN WILL THE WORLD STAND SILENT, NEVER AGAIN WILL THE WORLD ... FAIL TO ACT IN TIME TO PREVENT THIS TERRIBLE CRIME OF GENOCIDE.... WE MUST HARNESS THE OUTRAGE OF OUR MEMORIES TO STAMP OUT OPPRESSION WHEREVER IT EXISTS. WE MUST UNDERSTAND THAT HUMAN RIGHTS AND HUMAN DIGNITY ARE INDIVISIBLE.

—Jimmy Carter, 1979

THE THINGS I SAW BEGGAR THE IMAGINATION. THE VISUAL EVIDENCE AND THE VERBAL TESTIMONY WERE SO OVERPOWERING.... I HAVE REPORTED WHAT I SAW AND HEARD, BUT ONLY PART OF IT. FOR MOST OF IT, I HAVE NO WORDS. I MADE THE VISIT DELIBERATELY, IN ORDER TO BE IN A POSITION TO GIVE FIRST-HAND EVIDENCE OF THESE THINGS IF EVER, IN THE FUTURE, THERE DEVELOPS A TENDENCY TO CHARGE THESE ALLEGATIONS MERELY TO PROPAGANDA.

—General Dwight David Eisenhower, describing a visit to Ohrdruff Concentration Camp, April 12, 1945

HERE WE WILL LEARN MORE ABOUT THE MORAL COMPASS
BY WHICH WE NAVIGATE OUR LIVES AND BY WHICH COUNTRIES
WILL NAVIGATE THE FUTURE.

—George Bush, 1991

WE WHO DID NOT GO THEIR WAY OWE THEM THIS: WE MUST MAKE
SURE THAT THEIR DEATHS HAVE POSTHUMOUS MEANING.
WE MUST MAKE SURE THAT FROM NOW UNTIL THE END OF DAYS
HUMANKIND STARES THIS EVIL IN THE FACE ... AND ONLY THEN CAN
WE BE SURE THAT IT WILL NEVER ARISE AGAIN.

—Ronald Reagan, Cornerstone Dedication, October 5, 1988

THIS MUSEUM WILL TOUCH THE LIFE OF EVERYONE WHO ENTERS AND
LEAVE EVERYONE FOREVER CHANGED: A PLACE OF DEEP SADNESS AND A
SANCTUARY OF BRIGHT HOPE, AN ALLY OF EDUCATION AGAINST IGNO-
RANCE, OF HUMANITY AGAINST ARROGANCE, AN INVESTMENT IN A
SECURE FUTURE AGAINST WHATEVER INSANITY LURKS AHEAD. IF THIS
MUSEUM CAN MOBILIZE MORALITY, THEN THOSE WHO HAVE PERISHED
WILL THEREBY GAIN A MEASURE OF IMMORTALITY.

*—William J. Clinton, Dedication of the United States Holocaust
Memorial Museum, April 22, 1993*

DEDICATED IN GRATITUDE TO THE SUPREME COMMANDER OF ALLIED
FORCES IN EUROPE, GENERAL DWIGHT DAVID EISENHOWER, AND
THE VALIANT SOLDIERS VICTORIOUS IN BATTLE. THEY BROUGHT THE
THIRD REICH TO AN END, ENCOUNTERED ITS CONCENTRATION CAMPS,
LIBERATED THE SURVIVORS AND BORE WITNESS TO THE HOLOCAUST.

—Dedicatory Inscription

Interior

YOU ARE MY WITNESSES.

—The Holy Bible, *Isaiah 43:10*

THE GOVERNMENT OF THE UNITED STATES ... GIVES TO BIGOTRY
NO SANCTION, TO PERSECUTION NO ASSISTANCE.

—George Washington, 1790

ALL MEN ARE CREATED EQUAL.... THEY ARE ENDOWED BY THEIR
CREATOR WITH CERTAIN INALIENABLE RIGHTS.... AMONG THESE ARE
LIFE, LIBERTY, AND THE PURSUIT OF HAPPINESS.

—Declaration of Independence, 1776

Hall of Remembrance

WHAT HAVE YOU DONE? HARK, THY BROTHER'S BLOOD CRIES OUT
TO ME FROM THE GROUND!

—The Holy Bible, *Genesis 4:10*

I CALL HEAVEN AND EARTH TO WITNESS THIS DAY: I HAVE PUT
BEFORE YOU LIFE AND DEATH, BLESSING AND CURSE. CHOOSE LIFE—
THAT YOU AND YOUR OFFSPRING SHALL LIVE.

—The Holy Bible, *Deuteronomy 30:19*

ONLY GUARD YOURSELF AND GUARD YOUR SOUL CAREFULLY,
LEST YOU FORGET THE THINGS YOUR EYES SAW, AND LEST THESE
THINGS DEPART YOUR HEART ALL THE DAYS OF YOUR LIFE.
AND YOU SHALL MAKE THEM KNOWN TO YOUR CHILDREN,
AND TO YOUR CHILDREN'S CHILDREN.

—The Holy Bible, *Deuteronomy 6:9*

DEPARTMENT OF AGRICULTURE

*T*he Department of Agriculture was established in 1862 during the Civil War by the Lincoln administration. As the duties and size of the department expanded, Congress authorized funds at the turn of the century to construct a series of buildings for the department in Washington, D.C. The project commenced in 1903 and was completed in 1930 under the design of Rankin, Kellogg, and Crane of Philadelphia.

The department's main administration building is adjacent to the National Mall. During the construction of this building, from 1928 to 1930, land grant colleges and farmers' institutions were invited to submit recommendations for its inscriptions; the selected inscriptions are found on its northern exterior.

No other human occupation opens so wide a field for
profitable and agreeable combination of labor with
cultivated thought as agriculture.

—*Abraham Lincoln*

The husbandman that laboreth must
be first partaker of the fruits.

—The Holy Bible, *II Timothy 2:6*

With reference either to individual or national
welfare agriculture is of primary importance.

—*George Washington*

LIBRARY OF CONGRESS

The Library of Congress was established in 1800 to assemble books and publications for government and public use. When it was destroyed during the War of 1812, Thomas Jefferson sold his extensive personal collection to the government to form the new nucleus for the National Library.

In 1897, the Thomas Jefferson Building, the largest library of its day, was completed. Elaborately adorned with magnificent architectural details, sculpture, and paintings, the building is the work of J. J. Smithmeyer, Paul Pelez, and Edward P. Casey. Selections from world literature accompany many of the artistic decorations throughout the building.

In 1939, an additional Library of Congress building was completed and named after the United States' second president, John Adams. Known as the Library of Congress Annex, the structure was designed by Pierson and Wilson. The Thomas Jefferson Room of the Annex contains murals by Ezra Winter along with quotations from Jefferson.

A third structure, the James Madison Memorial Building, was built in 1980. Designed by Dewitt, Poor, and Shelton under the supervision of the Architect of the Capitol, it houses copyright offices and a legal library. It also contains the official memorial to James Madison, the United States' fourth president, who was also known as the "Father of the Constitution."

Thomas Jefferson Building, Ground Floor

A GOOD BOOK IS THE PRECIOUS LIFE BLOOD OF A MASTER SPIRIT.

—John Milton

BOOKS ARE THE TREASURED WEALTH OF THE WORLD.

—Henry David Thoreau

First Floor

E PLURIBUS UNUM.
(ONE OUT OF MANY.)

THE POETS, WHO ON EARTH HAVE MADE US HEIRS
OF TRUTH AND PURE DELIGHT BY HEAVENLY LAYS!

—William Wordsworth

KNOWLEDGE IS POWER.

—Francis Bacon

GIVE INSTRUCTION TO THOSE WHO CANNOT PROCURE IT
FOR THEMSELVES.

—Confucius

Original Librarian's Office

LITERA SCRIPTA MANET.
(THE WRITTEN WORD REMAINS.)

LIBER DILECTATIO ANIMAE.
(A BOOK IS THE SOUL'S DELIGHT.)

EFFICIUNT CLARUM STUDIO.
(THEY MAKE IT CLEAR BY STUDY.)

DULCES ANTE OMNIA MUSAE.
(SWEET ABOVE ALL THINGS ELSE ARE THE MUSES.)

IN TENEBRIS LUX.
(IN DARKNESS, LIGHT.)

The Rotunda

RELIGION

WHAT DOTH THE LORD REQUIRE OF THEE, BUT TO DO JUSTLY, TO
LOVE MERCY, AND TO WALK HUMBLY WITH THY GOD?

—The Holy Bible, *Micah 6:8*

COMMERCE

WE TASTE THE SPICES OF ARABIA YET NEVER FEEL THE
SCORCHING SUN WHICH BRINGS THEM FORTH.

—*Dudley North*

HISTORY

ONE GOD, ONE LAW, ONE ELEMENT,
AND ONE FAR-OFF DIVINE EVENT,
TO WHICH THE WHOLE CREATION MOVES.

—*Alfred, Lord Tennyson*

ART

As one lamp lights another, nor grows less,

so nobleness enkindleth nobleness.

—James Russell Lowell

PHILOSOPHY

The inquiry, knowledge, and belief of truth is the

sovereign good of human nature.

—Francis Bacon

POETRY

Hither, as to their fountain, other stars

repairing, in their golden urns draw light.

—John Milton

LAW

Of law there can be no less acknowledged than that

her voice is the harmony of the world.

—Richard Hooker

THE HEAVENS DECLARE THE GLORY OF GOD; AND THE
FIRMAMENT SHOWETH HIS HANDIWORK.

—The Holy Bible, *Psalms 19:1*

Second Floor

MAN RAISES BUT TIME WEIGHS.

—*Modern Greek Proverb*

BENEATH THE RULE OF MEN ENTIRELY GREAT,
THE PEN IS MIGHTIER THAN THE SWORD.

—*Bulwer Lytton*

THE NOBLEST MOTIVE IS THE PUBLIC GOOD.

—*Virgil*

THE TRUE UNIVERSITY OF THESE DAYS IS A COLLECTION OF BOOKS.

—*Thomas Carlyle*

NATURE IS THE ART OF GOD.

—*Sir Thomas Browne*

THERE IS NO WORK OF GENIUS WHICH HAS NOT BEEN THE
DELIGHT OF MANKIND.

—*James Russell Lowell*

IT IS THE MIND THAT MAKES THE MAN, AND OUR VIGOR
IS IN OUR IMMORTAL SOUL.

—*Ovid*

THEY ARE NEVER ALONE THAT ARE ACCOMPANIED WITH
NOBLE THOUGHTS.

—*Sir Philip Sidney*

MAN IS ONE WORLD,
AND HATH ANOTHER TO ATTEND HIM.

—*George Herbert*

TONGUES IN TREES, BOOKS IN THE RUNNING BROOKS,
SERMONS IN STONES, AND GOOD IN EVERYTHING.

—*William Shakespeare*

THE TRUE SHEKINAH IS MAN.

—*Saint John Chrysostom*

ONLY THE ACTIONS OF THE JUST
SMELL SWEET AND BLOSSOM IN THE DUST.

—James Shirley

ART IS LONG, AND TIME IS FLEETING.

—Henry Wadsworth Longfellow

THE HISTORY OF THE WORLD IS BUT THE
BIOGRAPHY OF GREAT MEN.

—Thomas Carlyle

BOOKS WILL SPEAK PLAIN WHEN COUNSELLORS BLANCH.

—Francis Bacon

GLORY IS ACQUIRED BY VIRTUE BUT PRESERVED BY LETTERS.

—Francesco Petrarch

THE FOUNDATION OF EVERY STATE IS THE
EDUCATION OF ITS YOUTH.

—Dionysius

THE CHIEF GLORY OF EVERY PEOPLE ARISES FROM ITS AUTHORS.

—*Samuel Johnson*

THERE IS ONE ONLY GOOD, NAMELY KNOWLEDGE,
AND ONE ONLY EVIL, NAMELY IGNORANCE.

—*Diogenes Laetius*

KNOWLEDGE COMES, BUT WISDOM LINGERS.

—*Alfred, Lord Tennyson*

WISDOM IS THE PRINCIPAL THING; THEREFORE GET WISDOM:
AND WITH ALL THY GETTING GET UNDERSTANDING.

—The Holy Bible, *Proverbs 4:7*

IGNORANCE IS THE CURSE OF GOD,
KNOWLEDGE THE WING WHEREWITH WE FLY TO HEAVEN.

—*William Shakespeare*

HOW CHARMING IS DIVINE PHILOSOPHY!

—*John Milton*

BOOKS MUST FOLLOW SCIENCES AND NOT SCIENCES BOOKS.

—*Francis Bacon*

IN BOOKS LIES THE SOUL OF THE WHOLE PAST TIME.

—*Thomas Carlyle*

READING MAKETH A FULL MAN, CONFERENCE A READY MAN,
AND WRITING AN EXACT MAN.

—*Francis Bacon*

WORDS ARE ALSO ACTIONS, AND ACTIONS ARE A KIND OF WORDS.

—*Ralph Waldo Emerson*

SCIENCE IS ORGANIZED KNOWLEDGE.

—*Herbert Spenser*

BEAUTY IS TRUTH, TRUTH BEAUTY.

—*John Keats*

Too low they build who build beneath the stars.

—*Edward Young*

There is but one temple in the Universe
and that is the Body of Man.

—*Novalis*

Beholding the bright countenance of Truth
In the quiet and still air
Of delightful studies.

—*John Milton*

The fault … is not in our stars,
But in ourselves, that we are underlings.

—*William Shakespeare*

The universal cause
Acts to one end, but acts by various laws.

—*Alexander Pope*

CREATION'S HEIR, THE WORLD, THE WORLD IS MINE!

—*Oliver Goldsmith*

VAIN, VERY VAIN, THE WEARY SEARCH TO FIND
THAT BLISS WHICH ONLY CENTRES IN THE MIND.

—*Oliver Goldsmith*

A LITTLE LEARNING IS A DANGEROUS THING;
DRINK DEEP, OR TASTE NOT THE PIERIAN SPRING.

—*Alexander Pope*

LEARNING IS BUT AN ADJUNCT TO OURSELF.

—*William Shakespeare*

STUDIES PERFECT NATURE AND ARE PERFECTED BY EXPERIENCE.

—*Francis Bacon*

DREAMS, BOOKS, ARE EACH A WORLD, AND BOOKS, WE KNOW,
ARE A SUBSTANTIAL WORLD, BOTH PURE AND GOOD.

—*William Wordsworth*

ALL ARE BUT PARTS OF ONE STUPENDOUS WHOLE,
WHOSE BODY NATURE IS, AND GOD THE SOUL.

—Alexander Pope

IN NATURE ALL IS USEFUL, ALL IS BEAUTIFUL.

—Ralph Waldo Emerson

THE FIRST CREATURE OF GOD WAS THE LIGHT OF SENSE; THE LAST
WAS THE LIGHT OF REASON.

—Francis Bacon

THE LIGHT SHINETH IN DARKNESS AND THE DARKNESS
COMPREHENDETH IT NOT.

—The Holy Bible, *John 1:5*

Dwells within the soul of every Artist
More than all his effort can express.
No great thinker ever lived and taught you
All the wonder that his soul received.
No true painter ever set on canvas
All the glorious vision he conceived.
No musician …
But be sure he heard, and strove to render
Feeble echoes of celestial strains.
No real poet ever wove in numbers
All his dreams.
Love and life united are twin mysteries,
Different yet the same.
Love may strive, but vain is the endeavor
All its boundless riches to unfold.
Art and love speak;
And their words must be
Like sighings of illimitable forests.

—Adelaide A. Procter

ORDER IS HEAVEN'S FIRST LAW.

—Alexander Pope

MEMORY IS THE TREASURE AND GUARDIAN OF ALL THINGS.

—Marcus Tullius Cicero

BEAUTY IS THE CREATOR OF THE UNIVERSE.

—Ralph Waldo Emerson

FOR A WEB BEGUN GOD SENDS THREAD.

—Old Proverb

THE WEB OF LIFE …
IS OF A MINGLED YARN, GOOD AND ILL TOGETHER.

—William Shakespeare

COMES THE BLIND FURY WITH TH' ABHORRED SHEARS
AND SLITS THE THIN-SPUN LIFE.

—John Milton

THIS IS THE STATE OF MAN: TO-DAY HE PUTS FORTH
THE TENDER LEAVES OF HOPES.
TOMORROW BLOSSOMS,
AND BEARS HIS BLUSHING HONOURS THICK UPON HIM;
THE THIRD DAY COMES A FROST ...
AND ... NIPS HIS ROOT,
AND THEN HE FALLS.

—*William Shakespeare*

Pavilion of the Seals

'TIS OUR TRUE POLICY TO STEER CLEAR OF PERMANENT ALLIANCE
WITH ANY PORTION OF THE FOREIGN WORLD.

—*George Washington*

LET OUR OBJECT BE OUR COUNTRY, OUR WHOLE COUNTRY,
AND NOTHING BUT OUR COUNTRY.

—*Daniel Webster*

THANK GOD I ALSO AM AN AMERICAN.

—*Daniel Webster*

Equal and exact justice to all men, of whatever state of persuasion, religious or political: commerce and honest friendship with all nations—entangling alliance with none.

—Thomas Jefferson

The agricultural interest of the country is connected with every other, and superior in importance to them all.

—Andrew Jackson

Let us have peace.

—Ulysses S. Grant

The aggregate happiness of society is, or ought to be, the end of all government.

—George Washington

To be prepared for war is one of the most effective means of preserving peace.

—George Washington

THAT THIS NATION, UNDER GOD, SHALL HAVE A NEW BIRTH OF FREEDOM; THAT GOVERNMENT OF THE PEOPLE, BY THE PEOPLE, FOR THE PEOPLE, SHALL NOT PERISH FROM THE EARTH.

—Abraham Lincoln

John Adams Building

(All quotations in the Thomas Jefferson Room of the John Adams Building are from Jefferson's writings.)

EDUCATE AND INFORM THE MASS OF THE PEOPLE. ENABLE THEM TO SEE THAT IT IS IN THEIR INTEREST TO PRESERVE PEACE AND ORDER AND THEY WILL PRESERVE THEM. ENLIGHTEN THE PEOPLE GENERALLY, AND TYRANNY AND OPPRESSIONS OF BODY AND MIND WILL VANISH LIKE EVIL SPIRITS AT THE DAWN OF DAY.

THE PEOPLE OF EVERY COUNTRY ARE THE ONLY SAFE GUARDIANS OF THEIR OWN RIGHTS AND ARE THE ONLY INSTRUMENTS WHICH CAN BE USED FOR THEIR DESTRUCTION. IT IS AN AXIOM IN MY MIND THAT OUR LIBERTY CAN NEVER BE SAFE BUT IN THE HANDS OF THE PEOPLE THEMSELVES THAT TOO OF THE PEOPLE WITH A CERTAIN DEGREE OF INSTRUCTION.

THE GROUND OF LIBERTY IS TO BE GAINED BY INCHES. WE MUST BE CONTENTED TO SECURE WHAT WE CAN GET FROM TIME TO TIME AND ETERNALLY PRESS FORWARD FOR WHAT IS YET TO GET. IT TAKES TIME TO PERSUADE MEN TO DO EVEN WHAT IS FOR THEIR OWN GOOD.

THOSE WHO LABOR IN THE EARTH ARE THE CHOSEN PEOPLE OF GOD
IF HE EVER HAD A CHOSEN PEOPLE WHOSE BREASTS HE HAS MADE
THE PECULIAR DEPOSITS FOR SUBSTANTIAL AND GENUINE VIRTUE.
IT IS THE FOCUS IN WHICH HE KEEPS ALIVE THAT SACRED FIRE
WHICH OTHERWISE MIGHT ESCAPE FROM THE EARTH.

THE EARTH BELONGS ALWAYS TO THE LIVING GENERATION. THEY
MAY MANAGE IT THEN AND WHAT PROCEEDS FROM IT AS THEY PLEASE
DURING THEIR USUFRUCT. THEY ARE MASTERS TOO OF THEIR OWN
PERSONS AND CONSEQUENTLY MAY GOVERN THEM AS THEY PLEASE.

James Madison Memorial Building, Exterior

(All inscriptions at the James Madison Memorial Building are attributable to Madison.)

KNOWLEDGE WILL FOREVER GOVERN IGNORANCE: AND A PEOPLE WHO
MEAN TO BE THEIR OWN GOVERNORS, MUST ARM THEMSELVES WITH
THE POWER WHICH KNOWLEDGE GIVES.

WHAT SPECTACLE CAN BE MORE EDIFYING OR MORE SEASONAL, THAN
THAT OF LIBERTY & LEARNING, EACH LEANING ON THE OTHER FOR
THEIR MUTUAL & SUREST SUPPORT?

LEARNED INSTITUTIONS OUGHT TO BE FAVORITE OBJECTS WITH
EVERY FREE PEOPLE. THEY THROW THAT LIGHT OVER THE PUBLIC
MIND WHICH IS THE BEST SECURITY AGAINST CRAFTY & DANGEROUS
ENCROACHMENTS ON THE PUBLIC LIBERTY.

THE HAPPY UNION OF THESE STATES IS A WONDER,
THEIR CONSTITUTION A MIRACLE: THEIR EXAMPLE THE HOPE
OF LIBERTY THROUGHOUT THE WORLD.

THE ESSENCE OF GOVERNMENT IS POWER;
AND POWER, LODGED AS IT MUST BE IN
HUMAN HANDS, WILL EVER BE
LIABLE TO ABUSE.

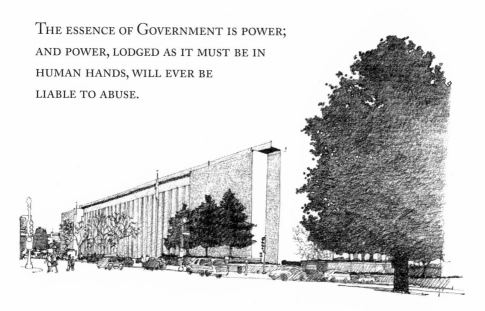

Equal laws protecting equal rights are ... the best guarantee of loyalty & love of country.

As a man is said to have a right to his property, he may be equally said to have a property in his rights.

War contains so much folly, as well as wickedness, that much is to be hoped from the progress of reason; and if anything is to be hoped every thing ought to be tried.

The free system of government we have established is so congenial with reason, with common sense, and with a universal feeling, that it must produce approbation and a desire of imitation, as avenues may be found for truth to the knowledge of nations.

The safety and happiness of society are the objects at which all political institutions aim, and to which all such institutions must be sacrificed.

The advice nearest to my heart and deepest in my convictions is that that union of the states be cherished and perpetuated.

FOLGER SHAKESPEARE LIBRARY

*D*edicated on April 23, 1932, the anniversary of Shakespeare's birth in 1564, the Folger Shakespeare Library contains an extensive collection of the playwright's works and other materials related to the English Renaissance.

The library was a gift to the American people from Henry Clay Folger and his wife Emily Jordan. Henry Folger (1857-1930) was a president and chairman of the board of Standard Oil Company of New York. He and his wife dedicated not only their financial resources, but also their time and personal collection to found the library.

The library contains more than a quarter-million theatrical materials, artifacts, notebooks, films, playbills, promptbooks, folios, scrapbooks, paintings, and costumes. It houses the world's largest collection of Shakespeare's writings as well as those of his contemporaries. It also houses an Elizabethan theater where plays are regularly held. The Great Hall displays special exhibits from the library's collections. Administered by Amherst College, the library attracts scholars worldwide. With the exception of the Reading Room, which is restricted to qualified individuals for research, the library is open to the public.

The library was designed by Dr. Paul Cret. It is located on Capitol Hill, one block southeast of the Supreme Court building. The building's inscriptions are either taken from Shakespeare's plays or reflect the praise of his fellow poets.

Exterior

THIS THEREFORE IS THE PRAISE OF SHAKESPEARE,
THAT HIS DRAMA IS THE MIRROUR OF LIFE.

—*Samuel Johnson*

HIS WIT CAN NO MORE LIE HID,
THEN IT COULD BE LOST.
READE HIM, THEREFORE;
AND AGAINE, AND AGAINE.

—*John Heminge and Henry Condell*

Thou art a moniment, without a tombe,
And art alive still, while thy booke doth live,
And we have wits to read, and praise to give.

—*Ben Jonson*

For wisedomes sake, a word that all men love.

—Love's Labour's Lost

Lord, what fooles these mortals be!

—A Midsummer-Night's Dream

Interior

I shower a welcome on ye; welcome all.

—Henry VIII

What needs my Shakespeare for his honor'd bones,
The labour of an age in piled stones,
Thou in our wonder and astonishment
Hast built thyself a live-long monument.

—*John Milton*

THERE IS NOT ANYTHING OF HUMAN TRIAL
THAT EVER LOVE DEPLORED OR SORROW KNEW,
NO GLAD FULFILLMENT AND NO SAD DENIAL.
BEYOND THE PICTURED TRUTH THAT SHAKESPEARE DREW.

—*William Winter*

THRICE HAPPY THE NATION THAT SHAKESPEARE HAS CHARM'D
MORE HAPPY THE BOSOME HIS GENIUS HAS WARM'D!
YE CHILDREN OF NATURE, OF FASHION, AND WHIM,
HE PAINTED YOU ALL, ALL JOIN TO PRAISE HIM.

—*David Garrick*

Reading Room

SHAKESPEARE IS FERTILITY, FORCE, EXUBERANCE, NO RETICENCE,
NO BINDING, NO ECONOMY, THE INORDINATE AND TRANQUIL
PRODIGALITY OF THE CREATOR.

—*Hugo*

I DO NOT REMEMBER THAT ANY BOOK OR PERSON OR EVENT EVER
PRODUCED SO GREAT AN EFFECT ON ME AS SHAKESPEARE'S PLAYS.

—*Johann Wolfgang von Goethe*

ENGLAND'S GENIUS FILLED ALL MEASURE
OF HEART AND SOUL, OF STRENGTH AND PLEASURE,
GAVE TO THE MIND ITS EMPEROR,
AND LIFE WAS LARGER THAN BEFORE:
NOR SEQUENT CENTURIES COULD HIT
ORBIT AND SUM OF SHAKESPEARE'S WIT.
THE MEN WHO LIVED WITH HIM BECAME
POETS, FOR THE AIR WAS FAME.

—*Ralph Waldo Emerson*

MARY MCLEOD BETHUNE MEMORIAL

*T*he Mary McLeod Bethune Memorial in Lincoln Park honors an indomitable and visionary African American woman. Born to former slaves in 1875, Bethune overcame the poverty and oppressive conditions of her youth to become a national advocate for racial progress and reform, especially in the area of education.

Shortly after completing her own formal education, Bethune founded the Daytona Literary and Industrial School for Training Negro Girls. Enrollment grew rapidly, and two decades later, in 1923, the school merged with the Cookman Institute. In 1931, it was renamed Bethune-Cookman College. To provide and widen educational opportunites for minority school children, Bethune aggressively appealed for funds on a national scale, raising the American consciousness of racial discrimination in the process. She became a personal friend and advisor to President and Mrs. Franklin D. Roosevelt and headed the Office of Minority Affairs during much of Roosevelt's adminstration.

Inscribed on the memorial is a summary of the legacy she left to African American children in her "Last Will and Testament," reflecting her deep belief in the dignity and worth of each individual. The memorial was dedicated in 1974 by the National Council of Negro Women. The statue of Bethune is by Robert Berks.

∾

Mary McLeod Bethune
1875-1955

I leave you love. I leave you hope. I leave you the challenge of developing confidence in one another. I leave you a thirst for education. I leave you a respect for the use of power. I leave you faith. I leave you racial diginity. I leave you also a desire to live harmoniously with your fellowman. I leave you, finally, a responsibility to our young people.

SUPREME COURT OF THE UNITED STATES

The Supreme Court is the highest judicial and appellate arm of the government, empowered to strike down laws not in harmony with the Constitution. Through its decisions, the Supreme Court gives interpretation and definition to that document.

Since its establishment, the Court has met in several places: New York (1790), Philadelphia (1791-1800), the United States Capitol (1800-1935), and at its current location east of the Capitol building. The inscription over the main entrance, "Equal Justice Under Law," is attributed to former Chief Justice Charles Evans Hughes. The origin of the inscription, "Justice The Guardian Of Liberty," on the building's east side, is unknown. The remaining inscriptions are found on the building's ground-floor level in a display honoring John Marshall. Marshall was chief justice during the formative years of the court, from 1801-1835, and his decisions, views, and writings on fundamental constitutional issues elevated the importance of the Supreme Court and greatly influenced the interpretation of basic constitutional questions.

In 1929, former President William H. Taft, who was then serving as Supreme Court chief justice (and remains the only American ever to have held both offices), encouraged Congress to provide funds to construct a permanent home for the Court. Cass Gilbert designed the building, which was completed in 1935.

(The following writings are from landmark decisions by Chief Justice John Marshall.)

NEVER FORGET THAT IT IS A CONSTITUTION WE ARE EXPOUNDING.

—*McCulloch v. Maryland, 1819*

THE PEOPLE MADE THE CONSTITUTION AND THE PEOPLE CAN UNMAKE
IT. IT IS A CREATURE OF THEIR WILL, AND LIVES ONLY BY THEIR WILL.

—*Cohens v. Virginia, 1821*

IT IS EMPHATICALLY THE PROVINCE AND DUTY OF THE JUDICIAL
DEPARTMENT TO SAY WHAT THE LAW IS.

—*Marbury v. Madison, 1803*

A CONSTITUTION IS FRAMED FOR AGES TO COME, AND IS DESIGNED
TO APPROACH IMMORTALITY AS NEARLY AS HUMAN INSTITUTIONS CAN
APPROACH IT. ITS COURSE CANNOT ALWAYS BE TRANQUIL.

—*Cohens v. Virginia, 1821*

LET THE END BE LEGITIMATE, LET IT BE WITHIN THE SCOPE
OF THE CONSTITUTION, AND ALL MEANS WHICH ARE
APPROPRIATE, WHICH ARE PLAINLY ADAPTED TO THAT END,
WHICH ARE NOT PROHIBITED, BUT CONSIST WITHIN THE LETTER
AND SPIRIT OF THE CONSTITUTION, ARE CONSTITUTIONAL.

—*McCulloch v. Maryland, 1819*

UNITED STATES CAPITOL

With its prominent hilltop setting, the United States Capitol is a striking national landmark, patterned after the architecture of the ancient Roman and Greek republics. The cornerstone of the building designed by William Thorton was laid by President George Washington in 1793. The structure was badly damaged by the British during the War of 1812, and its construction was not completed until 1826. By 1850, the Capitol was already overcrowded, and efforts began to enlarge the building. Even during the Civil War, when laborers were scarce, President Lincoln ordered that expansion efforts be continued because he recognized the Capitol's value as a symbol of national unification. Home to the House of Representatives and the Senate, the Capitol also housed the Library of Congress and the U. S. Supreme Court until 1897 and 1935, respectively.

In 1855, Constantino Brumidi, an Italian immigrant and master artist who had worked on the Vatican, was charged with the interior decoration of the Capitol. During the next 25 years, the gifted Brumidi painted walls and ceilings and exerted a lasting influence on the building's overall decor.

While inscriptions are found throughout the Capitol, most are located on the first floor corridors in its House Wing. Added during the nation's bicentennial in 1976, these writings accompany murals by Allyn Cox depicting milestones in United States history.

First Floor House Corridor

THE NATION BEHAVES WELL IF IT TREATS THE NATURAL RESOURCES
AS ASSETS WHICH IT MUST TURN OVER TO THE NEXT GENERATION
INCREASED, AND NOT IMPAIRED, IN VALUE.

—*Theodore Roosevelt*

ENLIGHTEN THE PEOPLE GENERALLY, AND TYRANNY AND
OPPRESSIONS OF BODY AND MIND WILL VANISH LIKE EVIL SPIRITS
AT THE DAWN OF DAY.

—*Thomas Jefferson*

HE THAT INVENTS A MACHINE AUGMENTS THE POWER OF A MAN AND
THE WELL BEING OF MANKIND.

—*Henry Ward Beecher*

LABOR IS DISCOVERED TO BE THE GRAND CONQUEROR ENRICHING AND
BUILDING UP NATIONS MORE SURELY THAN THE PROUDEST BATTLES.

—*William Ellery Channing*

WE DEFEND AND WE BUILD A WAY OF LIFE, NOT FOR AMERICA ALONE,
BUT FOR ALL MANKIND.

—*Franklin Delano Roosevelt*

WHENEVER A FREE MAN IS IN CHAINS WE ARE THREATENED ALSO.
WHOEVER IS FIGHTING FOR LIBERTY IS DEFENDING AMERICA.

—*William Allen White*

FREEDOM OF THOUGHT AND THE RIGHT OF PRIVATE
JUDGMENT IN MATTERS OF CONSCIENCE DIRECT
THEIR COURSE TO THIS HAPPY COUNTRY.

—*Samuel Adams*

WE MUST REMEMBER THAT ANY OPPRESSION, ANY INJUSTICE, ANY HATRED, IS A WEDGE DESIGNED TO ATTACK OUR CIVILIZATION.

—*Franklin Delano Roosevelt*

THE GREATEST DANGERS TO LIBERTY LURK IN INSIDIOUS ENCROACHMENT BY MEN OF ZEAL, WELL-MEANING BUT WITHOUT UNDERSTANDING.

—*Louis D. Brandeis*

LET US BUILD BROAD AND WIDE THESE FOUNDATIONS. LET THEM ABUT ONLY ON THE EVERLASTING SEAS.

—*Ignatius Donnelly*

WITHOUT FREEDOM OF THOUGHT, THERE CAN BE NO SUCH THING AS WISDOM; AND NO SUCH THING AS PUBLICK LIBERTY, WITHOUT FREEDOM OF SPEECH.

—*Benjamin Franklin*

WHEN TILLAGE BEGINS OTHER ARTS FOLLOW. THE FARMERS, THEREFORE, ARE THE FOUNDERS OF HUMAN CIVILIZATION.

—*Daniel Webster*

I HAVE BUT ONE LAMP BY WHICH MY FEET ARE GUIDED;
AND THAT IS THE LAMP OF EXPERIENCE.

—Patrick Henry

OUR GOVERNMENT CONCEIVED IN FREEDOM AND PURCHASED WITH
BLOOD CAN BE PRESERVED ONLY BY CONSTANT VIGILANCE.

—William Jennings Bryan

WHENEVER A PEOPLE OR AN INSTITUTION FORGET ITS HARD
BEGINNINGS, IT IS BEGINNING TO DECAY.

—Carl Sandburg

THE ONLY LEGITIMATE RIGHT TO GOVERN IS AN EXPRESS GRANT OF
POWER FROM THE GOVERNED.

—William Henry Harrison

MAN IS NOT MADE FOR THE STATE BUT THE STATE FOR MAN
AND IT DERIVES ITS JUST POWERS ONLY FROM THE CONSENT
OF THE GOVERNED.

—Thomas Jefferson

THIS GOVERNMENT, THE OFFSPRING OF OUR OWN CHOICE,
UNINFLUENCED AND UNAWED, HAS A JUST CLAIM TO YOUR
CONFIDENCE AND SUPPORT.

—*George Washington*

WE HAVE BUILT NO TEMPLE BUT THE CAPITOL. WE CONSULT NO
COMMON ORACLE BUT THE CONSTITUTION.

—*Rufus Choate*

HERE, SIR, THE PEOPLE GOVERN.

—*Alexander Hamilton*

YOU ARE THE RULERS AND THE RULED.

—*Adlai E. Stevenson*

LIBERTY AND UNION, ONE AND INSEPARABLE.

—*Daniel Webster*

ONE COUNTRY, ONE CONSTITUTION, ONE DESTINY.

—*Daniel Webster*

House Chamber

WE THE PEOPLE OF THE UNITED STATES, IN ORDER TO FORM A MORE
PERFECT UNION, ESTABLISH JUSTICE, INSURE DOMESTIC TRANQUILITY,
PROVIDE FOR THE COMMON DEFENSE, PROMOTE THE GENERAL
WELFARE, AND SECURE THE BLESSINGS OF OUR POSTERITY, DO ORDAIN
AND ESTABLISH THIS CONSTITUTION FOR THE UNITED STATES
OF AMERICA.

—Preamble of the Constitution of the United States

IN GOD WE TRUST.

LET US DEVELOPE THE RESOURCES OF OUR LAND, CALL FORTH ITS
POWERS, BUILD UP ITS INSTITUTIONS, PROMOTE ALL ITS GREAT
INTERESTS AND SEE WHETHER WE ALSO IN OUR DAY AND GENERATION
MAY NOT PERFORM SOMETHING WORTHY TO BE REMEMBERED.

—Daniel Webster

Senate Chamber

ANNUIT COEPTIS.
(GOD HAS FAVORED OUR UNDERTAKINGS.)

IN GOD WE TRUST.

Prayer Room

ANNUIT COEPTIS.
(GOD HAS FAVORED OUR UNDERTAKINGS.)

PRESERVE ME, O GOD: FOR IN THEE DO I PUT MY TRUST.

—The Holy Bible, *Psalm 16:1*

ROBERT A. TAFT MEMORIAL

*B*orn in 1889 in Cincinnati, Ohio, Robert A. Taft was the son of United States President and Chief Justice William Howard Taft. Upon completion of his studies at Yale and Harvard, the younger Taft returned to Cincinnati and practiced law.

Taft served in the Ohio legislature before his election to the United States Senate. Highly critical of Franklin Roosevelt's administration, he opposed the New Deal and favored more limited social programs. During his 14 years of service in the Senate, he became known as "Mr. Republican" because of the conservative values he held. Despite his distinguished standing in Congress, Taft failed in attempts to secure the Republican Party's nomination for president in 1940, 1948, and 1952. He remained active in the Senate until cancer claimed his life in 1953.

Less than two years after his death, Congress authorized the Robert A. Taft Memorial Foundation to erect a bell tower on the Capitol grounds in his memory. Built with private funds, the 100-foot tower is constructed of Tennessee marble and contains 27 bells cast in the Faccard Bell Foundry in France. The structure, which was dedicated in 1959, was designed by Douglas W. Orr. It is located immediately north of the Capitol. The inscriptions found on the bell tower walls are excerpts from the writings and speeches of Senator Taft.

✑

IF WE WISH TO MAKE DEMOCRACY PERMANENT IN THIS COUNTRY, LET US ABIDE BY THE FUNDAMENTAL PRINCIPLES LAID DOWN IN THE CONSTITUTION. LET US SEE THAT THE STATE IS THE SERVANT OF ITS PEOPLE AND THAT THE PEOPLE ARE NOT SERVANTS OF THE STATE.

LIBERTY HAS BEEN THE KEY TO OUR PROGRESS IN THE PAST, AND IS
THE KEY TO OUR PROGRESS IN THE FUTURE. IF WE CAN PRESERVE
LIBERTY IN ALL ITS ESSENTIALS, THERE IS NO LIMIT TO THE FUTURE
OF THE AMERICAN PEOPLE.

UNION STATION

*U*nion Station, located at the northern base of Capitol Hill, was constructed to serve as a passenger rail port and gateway to the capital. It opened to the public in 1907. Designed by Daniel H. Burnham, the station's entrance is decorated with sculptures, archways, and fountains, and was immediately acclaimed for its architectural beauty.

Union Station experienced its greatest use during World War II. However, after the war, ridership steadily declined, and by the late 1960s, the station was offered for sale to the federal government. Over the next decade, various complications prevented the sale from occurring, and because funds were scarce, few improvements were made. Finally, the station fell into such poor condition that its interior was closed due to public safety concerns.

Recognizing the historic and transportation value of the facility, Congress enacted the Union Station Redevelopment Act in 1981. Renovation was completed in 1988 at a cost of $160 million. Original architectural details were preserved wherever possible throughout the building. The station accommodates approximately 20,000 passengers daily. It also contains numerous restaurants, shops, and movie theaters.

The inscriptions at Union Station are located on the southern exterior attics. They accompany six allegorical figures that represent Fire, Electricity, Freedom, Imagination, Mechanics, and Agriculture. They were either composed or selected by Dr. Charles W. Eliot, a former president of Harvard University.

Exterior

FIRE—GREATEST OF DISCOVERIES,
ENABLING MAN TO LIVE IN VARIOUS CLIMATES
USE MANY FOODS—AND COMPEL
THE FORCES OF NATURE TO DO HIS WORK.

ELECTRICITY—CARRIER OF LIGHT AND POWER
DEVOURER OF TIME AND SPACE—BEARER
OF HUMAN SPEECH OVER LAND AND SEA
GREAT SERVANT OF MAN, ITSELF UNKNOWN.

THOU HAST PUT ALL THINGS UNDER HIS FEET.
—The Holy Bible, *Psalms 8:6*

SWEETENER OF HUT AND OF HALL
BRINGER OF LIFE OUT OF NAUGHT
FREEDOM O FAIREST OF ALL
THE DAUGHTERS OF TIME AND THOUGHT.

MAN'S IMAGINATION HAS CONCEIVED ALL
NUMBERS AND LETTERS—ALL TOOLS, VESSELS
AND SHELTERS—EVERY ART AND TRADE—ALL
PHILOSOPHY AND POETRY AND ALL POLITIES.

THE TRUTH SHALL MAKE YOU FREE.

—The Holy Bible, *John 8:32*

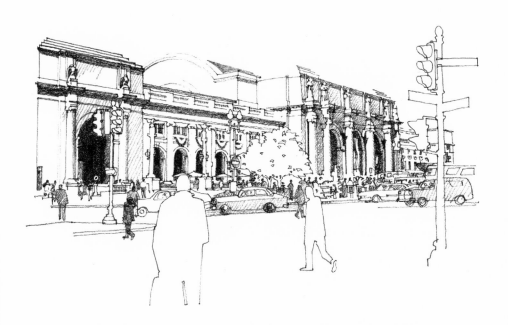

THE FARM—BEST HOME OF THE FAMILY—MAIN
SOURCE OF NATIONAL WEALTH—FOUNDATION OF
CIVILIZED SOCIETY—THE NATURAL PROVIDENCE.

THE OLD MECHANIC ARTS—CONTROLLING NEW
FORCES—BUILD NEW HIGHWAYS FOR GOODS
AND MEN—OVERRIDE THE OCEAN—AND MAKE
THE VERY ETHER CARRY HUMAN THOUGHT.

THE DESERT SHALL REJOICE AND BLOSSOM AS THE ROSE.

—The Holy Bible, *Isaiah 35:1*

HE THAT WOULD BRING HOME THE WEALTH OF THE INDIES MUST
CARRY THE WEALTH OF THE INDIES WITH HIM. SO IT IS IN
TRAVELLING—A MAN MUST CARRY KNOWLEDGE WITH HIM IF HE
WOULD BRING HOME KNOWLEDGE.

—*Samuel Johnson*

LET ALL THE ENDS THOU AIMEST AT
BE THY COUNTRY'S, THY GOD'S, AND TRUTH'S.

—*William Shakespeare*

BE NOBLE,
AND THE NOBLENESS THAT LIES
IN OTHER MEN, SLEEPING BUT NEVER DEAD,
WILL RISE IN MAJESTY TO MEET THINE OWN.

—James Russell Lowell

WELCOME THE COMING, SPEED THE PARTING GUEST.

—Alexander Pope

VIRTUE ALONE IS SWEET SOCIETY
IT KEEPS THE KEY TO ALL HEROIC HEARTS
AND OPENS YOU A WELCOME IN THEM ALL.

—Ralph Waldo Emerson

NATIONAL POSTAL MUSEUM

*I*n 1993, the Smithsonian Institution opened the National Postal Museum, which provides a rich history of mail delivery in the United States. Through an extensive collection of stamps, cards, letters, and artifacts, the museum explains the progressive role the postal service has played in the social and economic development of the country. Beginning with the pre-Revolutionary period, the museum covers significant milestones in the evolution of mail delivery. The history of postal innovations—such as "home delivery," which emerged during the Civil War when officials felt that it was better for news of a soldier's death to be received at home rather than at a post office window—is presented in six major exhibition galleries. These galleries also display the various forms of transportation and automation that have been used over the past several centuries to move the mail.

Located next to Union Station, the National Postal Museum is housed in the former Washington City Post Office building. Designed by Daniel H. Burnham, the building was completed in 1914 and was one of the country's most elaborate and advanced postal facilities in its day. The building's exterior inscriptions were composed by Dr. Charles W. Eliot, a former president of Harvard University, and were edited by President Woodrow Wilson.

❧

MESSENGER OF SYMPATHY AND LOVE
SERVANT OF PARTED FRIENDS
CONSOLER OF THE LONELY
BOND OF THE SCATTERED FAMILY
ENLARGER OF THE COMMON LIFE

CARRIER OF NEWS AND KNOWLEDGE
INSTRUMENT OF TRADE AND INDUSTRY
PROMOTER OF MUTUAL ACQUAINTANCE
OF PEACE AND GOOD WILL
AMONG MEN AND NATIONS.

NATIONAL ARCHIVES

*D*esigned by John Russell Pope and dedicated in 1935, the National Archives building houses extensive records pertaining to the civil, political, military, legislative, and diplomatic activities of the country. The most notable documents stored here are the Charters of Freedom: the Declaration of Independence, the Constitution of the United States, and the Bill of Rights. One of the four existing copies of the British Magna Carta is also displayed in the building because of its influence on the formation of American government.

These priceless artifacts are permanently sealed in uniquely designed exhibition cases which control gas and vapor concentrations. Each night, the documents are lowered and secured in a 55-ton reinforced concrete-and-steel vault below the Exhibition Hall Floor.

The National Archives is charged with maintaining a lasting representative account of the United States. To do so, archives officials conduct an extensive, ongoing review of materials to determine what should be preserved. Among the billions of items the National Archives has on record are textual material, still pictures, aerial photographs, motion picture film, sound recordings, and maps. The National Archives also publishes the *Federal Register* and manages presidential libraries throughout the country.

Exterior

THIS BUILDING HOLDS IN TRUST THE RECORDS OF OUR
NATIONAL LIFE AND SYMBOLIZES OUR FAITH IN THE
PERMANENCY OF OUR NATIONAL INSTITUTION.

THE TIES THAT BIND THE LIVES OF OUR PEOPLE IN ONE INDISSOLUBLE
UNION ARE PERPETUATED IN THE ARCHIVES OF OUR GOVERNMENT
AND TO THEIR CUSTODY THIS BUILDING IS DEDICATED.

—Dedicatory Inscription

THE GLORY AND ROMANCE OF OUR HISTORY ARE HERE PRESERVED
IN THE CHRONICLES OF THOSE WHO CONCEIVED AND BUILDED
THE STRUCTURE OF OUR NATION.

—Dedicatory Inscription

STUDY THE PAST.

THE HERITAGE OF THE PAST IS THE SEED THAT BRINGS
FORTH THE HARVEST OF THE FUTURE.

—James Earle Fraser, Charles Moore, and Dr. R.W.D. O'Connor

ETERNAL VIGILANCE IS THE PRICE OF LIBERTY.

—John P. Curran

WHAT IS PAST IS PROLOGUE.

—William Shakespeare

DEPARTMENT OF JUSTICE

The Department of Justice building is located in the Federal Triangle, a triangular area between Pennsylvania Avenue, 15th Street, and Constitution Avenue that also includes the Department of Commerce building, the former Post Office Department, the Internal Revenue Service, the National Archives, and the Federal Trade Commission. The Department of Justice building was designed by Zantzinger, Borie, and Medary of Philadelphia and was completed in 1934. The building comprises an entire city block and is designed as a hollow square with a series of interior courtyards. In its Great Court is a life-size memorial to Robert F. Kennedy, who served as United States attorney general from 1961 to 1964. The rectangular pedestal that holds the bust is missing its upper left corner, symbolic of Kennedy's life cut short in 1968.

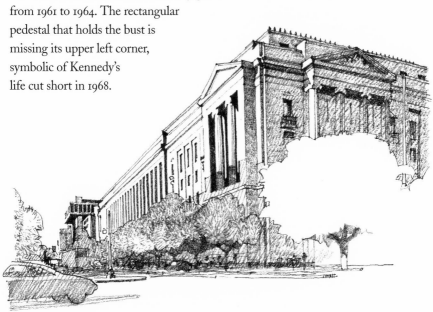

The building's ornamentations, fountains, statues, mosaics, and murals reflect the work of many American artists. Inscriptions appear on the building's exterior entrances, windows, and attic panels. Except for the quotation from Daniel Webster, all are attributed to Carl Paul Jennewein, who was selected to coordinate the sculptural decoration of the building.

☙

JUSTICE IS THE GREAT INTEREST OF MAN ON EARTH.
WHEREVER HER TEMPLE STANDS THERE IS A FOUNDATION FOR
SOCIAL SECURITY, GENERAL HAPPINESS, AND THE
IMPROVEMENT AND PROGRESS OF OUR RACE.

—Daniel Webster

ABOVE ALL STATUES IS THE FIGURE OF JUSTICE.

THE PLACE OF JUSTICE IS A HALLOWED PLACE.

JUSTICE IS SET AND CONSTANT PURPOSE TO RENDER
EVERY MAN HIS DUE.

JUSTICE TO EACH IS THE GOOD OF ALL.

JUSTICE IN THE LIFE AND CONDUCT OF THE STATE IS POSSIBLE ONLY AS
FIRST IT RESIDES IN THE HEARTS AND SOULS OF THE CITIZENS.

Lege atque ordine omnia fiunt.
(Everything is created by Law and Order.)

Justice is founded in the rights bestowed by nature upon
man. Liberty is maintained in security of justice.

The common law is the will of mankind: issuing from
the life of the people, framed through mutual confidence,
sanctioned by the light of reason.

Justice alone sustains society: founded on the principles
of right, expressed in the national laws, administered
by public officers.

No free government can survive that is not based
on the supremacy of law.

Where law ends tyranny begins.

Law alone can give us freedom.

FORMER POST OFFICE DEPARTMENT BUILDING

*I*n 1934, construction was completed on the Post Office Department building, designed by Delano and Aldrich of New York. This building, which is located on Pennsylvania Avenue between 12th and 13th Streets, housed postal headquarters until 1971. The cornerstone of the structure was set with the same trowel used by George Washington when he laid the cornerstone of the U. S. Capitol. James A. Farley was the first postmaster general to work in the building after its construction; his spacious walnut-paneled office with two fireplaces and oak floors was considered by many to be the most beautiful cabinet member's office in Washington. The office is now used for meetings and various government functions.

While the building still contains a postal station, it primarily houses Deparment of the Treasury staff and other government officials. The building's inscription was taken from an annual report submitted by Postmaster General Joseph Holt in 1859. Also found on the building's walls are inscriptions that list milestones in American postal history.

❧

The Post Office Department, in its ceaseless labors, pervades every channel of commerce and every theatre of human enterprise, and, while visiting, as it does kindly, every fireside, mingles with the throbbings of almost every heart in the land. In the amplitude of its beneficence, it ministers to all climes, and creeds, all pursuits, with the same eager readiness and equal fullness of fidelity. It is the delicate ear trump through which alike nations and families and isolated individuals whisper their joys and their sorrows, their convictions and their sympathies, to all who listen for their coming.

FREEDOM PLAZA

"*P*lan of the City of Washington, in the Territory of Columbia, ceded by the States of Virginia and Maryland to the United States of America, and by them established as the Seat of their Government after the Year MDCCC." Freedom Plaza contains this dedicatory inscription, along with dozens of quotations relating to the history and development of the city. Also inscribed in the plaza floor are maps, seals, charters, plans, and likenesses of other documents relating to its history, as well as a miniature-scale grid of Pennsylvania Avenue and the original plans for the Capitol and the President's House.

Dedicated in 1980 as Western Plaza, the public square is a large, raised terrace located on Pennsylvania Avenue between 13th and 14th Streets. In 1988, a time capsule containing historical items highlighting the life and work of Dr. Martin Luther King, Jr., was embedded in Western Plaza. That year Congress also authorized the renaming of the plaza to "Freedom Plaza" in honor of Dr. King's memory.

Freedom Plaza is the site of numerous artistic and cultural events, festivals, and activities throughout the year. It was designed by Robert Venturi under the direction of the Pennsylvania Avenue Development Corporation.

❧

WASHINGTON ... IS THE SYMBOL OF AMERICA. BY ITS DIGNITY
AND ARCHITECTURAL INSPIRATION ... WE ENCOURAGE THAT
ELEVATION OF THOUGHT AND CHARACTER WHICH COMES
FROM A GREAT ARCHITECTURE.

–Herbert Hoover, 1929

EVERY DEDICATED AMERICAN COULD BE PROUD THAT A DYNAMIC
EXPERIENCE OF DEMOCRACY IN HIS NATION'S CAPITAL HAD
BEEN MADE VISIBLE TO THE WORLD.

—Martin Luther King, Jr., 1963

THERE ARE TWO WASHINGTONS—POLITICAL WASHINGTON AND
THE REAL WASHINGTON MADE UP OF FRIENDS AND NEIGHBORS.

—Benjamin McKelway, 1951

THE CITY OF WASHINGTON IS IN SOME RESPECTS SELF CONTAINED,
AND IT IS EASY THERE TO FORGET WHAT THE REST OF THE UNITED
STATES IS THINKING ABOUT.

—Woodrow Wilson, 1913

I WENT TO WASHINGTON AS EVERYBODY GOES THERE, PREPARED TO
SEE EVERYTHING DONE WITH SOME FURTIVE INTENTION, BUT I WAS
DISAPPOINTED—PLEASANTLY DISAPPOINTED.

—Walt Whitman, 1888

IN WASHINGTON THERE IS NO LIFE APART FROM THE GOVERNMENT AND POLITICS: IT IS OUR DAILY BREAD; IT IS THE THREAD WHICH RUNS THROUGH THE WOOF AND WARP OF OUR LIVES; IT COLORS EVERYTHING.

—A. Maurice Low, 1900

WHO DOES NOT FEEL THAT, WHEN PRESIDENT WASHINGTON LAID HIS HAND ON THE FOUNDATION OF THE FIRST CAPITOL, HE PERFORMED A GREAT WORK OF PERPETUATION OF THE UNION AND THE CONSTITUTION?

—Daniel Webster, 1851

IT IS OUR NATIONAL CENTER. IT BELONGS TO US, AND WHETHER IT IS MEAN OR MAJESTIC, WHETHER ARRAYED IN GLORY OR COVERED WITH SHAME, WE CANNOT BUT SHARE ITS CHARACTER AND ITS DESTINY.

—Frederick Douglass, 1877

THE CAPITAL OF THE GREAT REPUBLIC GATHERED ITS PEOPLE FROM THE FOUR WINDS OF HEAVEN, AND SO THE MANNERS, THE FACES AND THE FASHIONS THERE, PRESENTED A VARIETY THAT WAS INFINITE.

—Mark Twain, 1874

WITH THE WORLD WAR WASHINGTON CHANGED ITS CHARACTER
FOREVER.... IN A MOMENT ... IT BECAME THE HEART OF THE WORLD,
THE WORLD COUNTING ITS EVERY PULSATION.

—*Marietta Minnigerode Andrews, 1928*

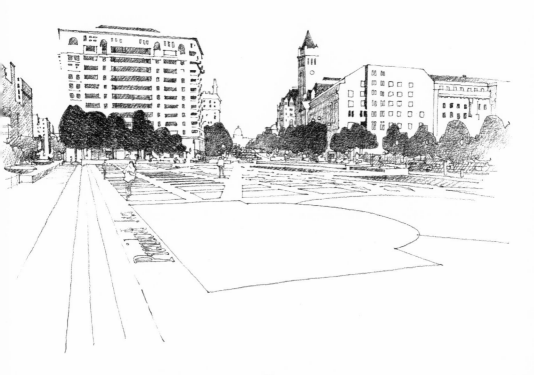

A CENTURY HENCE, IF THIS COUNTRY KEEPS UNITED, IT WILL
PRODUCE A CITY THOUGH NOT SO LARGE AS LONDON, YET OF
MAGNITUDE INFERIOR TO FEW OTHERS IN EUROPE.

—George Washington, 1789

OUR CAPITAL CITY, BORN IN THE POTOMAC MARSHLANDS,
HAS GROWN BY FEEDING ON AN INDESTRUCTIBLE IDEA.

—Joel Sayre, 1950

NO NATION HAD EVER BEFORE THE OPPORTUNITY OFFERED THEM
OF DELIBERATELY DECIDING ON THE SPOT WHERE THEIR
CAPITAL CITY SHOULD BE FIXED.

—Pierre Charles L'Enfant, 1789

WHATEVER WE ARE LOOKING FOR, WE COME TO WASHINGTON IN
MILLIONS TO STAND IN SILENCE AND TRY TO FIND IT.

—Bruce Catton, 1959

WASHINGTON IS NO PLACE IN WHICH TO CARRY OUT INVENTIONS.

—Alexander Graham Bell, 1887

WHAT YOU WANT IS TO HAVE A CITY WHICH EVERYONE WHO COMES
FROM MAINE, TEXAS, FLORIDA, ARKANSAS, OR OREGON CAN ADMIRE
AS BEING SOMETHING FINER AND MORE BEAUTIFUL THAN HE HAD
EVER DREAMED OF BEFORE.

—James Bryce, 1913

MAY THE SPIRIT WHICH ANIMATED THE GREAT FOUNDER OF THIS
CITY DESCEND TO FUTURE GENERATIONS.

—John Adams, 1800

THE SUM OF ALL KNOWN REVERENCE I ADD UP IN YOU, WHOEVER YOU
ARE, THE PRESIDENT IS THERE IN THE WHITE HOUSE FOR YOU,
IT IS NOT YOU WHO ARE HERE FOR HIM.

—Walt Whitman, 1855

NEVER, TIL THE CAPITAL HAD COST THE LIFE OF THE BEAUTIFUL AND
THE BRAVE OF OUR LAND, DID IT BECOME TO THE HEART OF THE
AMERICAN CITIZEN OF THE NINETEENTH CENTURY THE OBJECT OF
PERSONAL LOVE THAT IT WAS TO GEORGE WASHINGTON.

—Mary Clemmer Ames, circa 1874

WHEREVER THE AMERICAN CITIZEN MAY BE A STRANGER,
HE IS AT HOME HERE.

—*Frederick Douglass, 1877*

WASHINGTON HAS CERTAINLY AN AIR OF MORE MAGNIFICENCE
THAN ANY OTHER AMERICAN TOWN. IT IS MEAN IN DETAIL, BUT
THE OUTLINE HAS A CERTAIN GRANDEUR ABOUT IT.

—*James Fenimore Cooper, 1838*

I HAVE NEVER DOUBTED THE CONSTITUTIONAL AUTHORITY OF
CONGRESS TO ABOLISH SLAVERY IN THIS DISTRICT; AND I HAVE
EVER DESIRED TO SEE THE NATIONAL CAPITAL FREED FROM THE
INSTITUTION IN SOME SATISFACTORY WAY.

—*Abraham Lincoln, 1862*

BUT, TAKING IT ALL IN ALL AND AFTER ALL, NEGRO LIFE IN
WASHINGTON IS A PROMISE RATHER THAN A FULFILLMENT.
BUT IT IS WORTHY OF NOTE FOR THE REALLY EXCELLENT
THINGS WHICH ARE PROMISED.

—*Paul Laurence Dunbar, 1900*

THERE SEEMS REASON TO ANTICIPATE THAT IN TIME OUR CAPITAL
CITY OF WASHINGTON WILL COME TO BE AS WELL KNOWN AS
A CENTRE OF LITERATURE AND ART, AS IT IS NOW RECOGNIZED AS
THE CENTRE OF STATESMANSHIP, LAW AND SCIENCE.

—I. Edwards Clarke, 1899

ALL'S QUIET ALONG THE POTOMAC TO-NIGHT,
WHERE THE SOLDIERS LIE PEACEFULLY DREAMING:
THEIR TENTS IN THE RAYS OF THE CLEAR AUTUMN MOON,
IN THE LIGHT OF THE WATCH FIRES ARE GLEAMING.

—Ethel Beers, 1879

I AM HERE NOW AND HAVE SEEN YOUR PEOPLE, YOUR HOUSES, YOUR
VESSELS ON THE BIG LAKE, AND GREAT MANY WONDERFUL THINGS
FAR BEYOND MY COMPREHENSION, WHICH APPEAR TO HAVE BEEN
MADE BY THE GREAT SPIRIT AND PLACED IN YOUR HANDS.

—Sharitarish Pawnee, 1822

IT IS SOMETHING CALLED THE CITY OF MAGNIFICENT DISTANCES,
BUT IT MIGHT WITH GREATER PROPRIETY BE TERMED THE
CITY OF MAGNIFICENT INTENTIONS.

—Charles Dickens, 1842

THE GRAND AVENUE CONNECTING BOTH THE PALACE AND THE
FEDERAL HOUSE WILL BE MOST SIGNIFICANT AND MOST CONVENIENT.

—*Thomas Jefferson, 1791*

ONE OF THESE DAYS THIS WILL BE A VERY GREAT CITY IF
NOTHING HAPPENS TO IT.

—*Henry Adams, 1877*

IF WASHINGTON SHOULD EVEN GROW TO BE A GREAT CITY, THE
OUTLOOK FROM THE CAPITOL WILL BE UNSURPASSED IN THE
WORLD. NOW AT SUNSET I SEEMED TO LOOK WESTWARD FAR INTO
THE HEART OF THE CONTINENT FROM THIS COMMANDING POSITION.

—*Ralph Waldo Emerson, 1843*

WASHINGTON … ENORMOUS SPACES, HUNDREDS OF MILES OF
ASPHALTE, A CHARMING CLIMATE AND THE MOST ENTERTAINING
SOCIETY IN AMERICA.

—*Henry James, 1882*

THERE IS NOT A STREET IN ANY CITY IN THIS COUNTRY ENTITLED
TO THE EMINENT DISTINCTION WHICH CROWNS THE HISTORY OF
PENNSYLVANIA AVENUE.

—Samuel C. Busey, 1898

WASHINGTON WAS PLANNED AS A CITY OF IDEALS.

—Charles Moore, 1930

WASHINGTON WAS PLANNED BY MEN OF IMAGINATION, WHO
STOOD AMID THE SWAMPS AND BRIAR PATCHES AT THE HEAD OF
NAVIGATION ON THE POTOMAC AND VISUALIZED A CITY
OF HALF A MILLION POPULATION.

—George Rothwell Brown, 1930

HOW SHALL YOU ACT THE NATURAL MAN IN THIS INVENTED CITY,
NEITHER ROME NOR HOME?

—Ernest Kroll, 1952

LIVING IN CONTEMPORARY WASHINGTON, CAUGHT LITERALLY AND PHYSICALLY IN L'ENFANT'S DREAM, AND ENCOUNTERING ON EVERY HAND THE BRAVE MOMENTOS OF WASHINGTON, JEFFERSON, JACKSON, LINCOLN AND ROOSEVELT, IS TO LIVE AS CLOSE AS POSSIBLE TO BOTH THE SOURCE AND THE CLIMAX OF ONE OF THE MAJOR SEQUENCES OF THE HUMAN STORY.

—George Sessions Perry, 1946

MORE THAN ANY OTHER CITY—MORE THAN ANY OTHER REGION, THE NATION'S CAPITAL SHOULD REPRESENT THE FINEST IN LIVING ENVIRONMENT WHICH AMERICA CAN PLAN AND BUILD.

—John F. Kennedy, 1961

I STILL HAVE A DREAM. IT IS A DREAM DEEPLY ROOTED IN THE AMERICAN DREAM AND, IF AMERICA IS TO BE A GREAT NATION, THIS MUST BECOME TRUE. LET FREEDOM RING FROM EVERY HILL…. FROM EVERY MOUNTAINSIDE, LET FREEDOM RING.

—Martin Luther King, Jr., 1963

DEPARTMENT OF COMMERCE

ℐn 1903, President Theodore Roosevelt signed into law a measure that created the Department of Commerce and Labor. A decade later, this department was separated into two different entities. The Department of Commerce was charged with managing foreign and domestic commerce matters, administering lighthouse services, taking the national census, making coastal and geodetic surveys, collecting and publishing commerce statistics, and investigating markets for American products. The Department is also responsible for the National Ocean Service, the National Weather Service, and the Patent and Trademark Office.

The site of the Department of Commerce building was originally used for grazing cattle. Construction commenced in 1927, and when the structure was completed in 1932, it was the largest office complex in the world.

The building, which was designed by the New York architectural firm York and Sawyer, was named after Herbert Clark Hoover, a former secretary of commerce. The building contains a series of internal courtyards and is located on the western edge of the Federal Triangle. Inscriptions are found along the exterior facades and entrances of the building.

༂

THE DEPARTMENT OF COMMERCE ASSEMBLES HERE THE FORCES DE-SIGNED BY CONGRESS TO ADVANCE THE INTERESTS OF INDUSTRY AND TRADE. THROUGH EXPERIMENTAL RESEARCH, THE DISSEMINATION OF KNOWLEDGE, AND ADMINISTRATIVE VIGILANCE IT STIMULATES THE PROGRESS OF AMERICA UPON LAND AND SEA AND IN THE AIR AND THEREBY SPEEDS THE NATION IN THE MARCH OF MANKIND.

—Dedicatory Inscription

THE INSPIRATION THAT GUIDED OUR FOREFATHERS LED THEM TO SE-CURE ABOVE ALL THINGS THE UNITY OF OUR COUNTRY. WE REST UPON GOVERNMENT BY CONSENT OF THE GOVERNED, AND THE POLITICAL OR-DER OF THE UNITED STATES IS THE EXPRESSION OF A PATRIOTIC IDEAL WHICH WELDS TOGETHER ALL THE ELEMENTS OF OUR NATIONAL ENERGY, PROMOTING THE ORGANIZATION THAT FOSTERS INDIVIDUAL INITIATIVE. WITHIN THIS EDIFICE ARE ESTABLISHED AGENCIES THAT HAVE BEEN CREATED TO BUTTRESS THE LIFE OF THE PEOPLE, TO CLARIFY

THEIR PROBLEMS AND COORDINATE THEIR RESOURCES, SEEKING TO LIGHTEN BURDENS WITHOUT LESSENING THE RESPONSIBILITY OF THE CITIZEN. IN SERVING ONE AND ALL, THEY ARE DEDICATED TO THE PURPOSE OF THE FOUNDERS AND TO THE HIGHEST HOPES OF THE FUTURE WITH THEIR LOYAL ADMINISTRATION GIVEN TO THE INTEGRITY AND WELFARE OF THE NATION.

—Dedicatory Inscription

BASED UPON FOUNDATIONS OF DEVOTION AND LABOR, THE UNITED STATES IS ENRICHED BY OTHER GOLDEN THREADS IN THE GENIUS OF ITS PEOPLE. INVENTIVE DARING ILLUMINES THEIR DILIGENCE. ADVENTUROUS ARDOR INVIGORATES THE WORK OF THEIR HANDS. UNDER GOVERNMENTAL GUARDIANSHIP THEIR IDEALS AND THEIR ACTIVITIES ARE ASSURED THE LIBERTY THAT IS THE SOUL OF ACHIEVEMENT.

—Dedicatory Inscription

THE PATENT SYSTEM ADDED THE FUEL OF INTEREST
TO THE FIRE OF GENIUS.

—Abraham Lincoln

LET US RAISE A STANDARD TO WHICH THE WISE
AND HONEST CAN REPAIR.

—*George Washington*

COMMERCE DEFIES EVERY WIND, OUTRIDES EVERY TEMPEST,
AND INVADES EVERY ZONE.

—*George Bancroft*

COMMERCE AMONG NATIONS SHOULD BE FAIR AND EQUITABLE.

—*Benjamin Franklin*

CULTIVATE PEACE AND COMMERCE WITH ALL.

—*Thomas Jefferson*

NATIONAL MUSEUM OF AMERICAN HISTORY

*T*he National Museum of American History is just one of many Smithsonian Institution museums and galleries located on the National Mall at the western foot of Capitol Hill. The inscriptions found on the building pay tribute to the contribution and vision of James Smithson. The Smithsonian Institution was founded by Congress in 1847 with funds from the distinguished British scientist's estate.

Established "for the increase and diffusion of knowledge among men," the Institution is an impressive collection of cultural, historic, and scientific institutes. The 16 museums and galleries of the Smithsonian, located in Washington, D.C., and New York City, make it the most extensive museum complex in the world today.

❧

EVERYMAN IS A VALUABLE MEMBER OF SOCIETY WHO, BY HIS OBSERVATIONS, RESEARCHES, AND EXPERIENCES, PROCURES KNOWLEDGE FOR MEN.... IT IS IN HIS KNOWLEDGE THAT MAN HAS FOUND HIS GREATNESS AND HIS HAPPINESS, THE HIGH SUPERIORITY WHICH HE HOLDS OVER THE OTHER ANIMALS WHO INHABIT THE EARTH WITH HIM, AND CONSEQUENTLY NO IGNORANCE IS PROBABLY WITHOUT LOSS TO HIM, NO ERROR WITHOUT EVIL.... THE PARTICLE AND THE PLANET ARE SUBJECT TO THE SAME LAWS, AND WHAT IS LEARNED OF ONE WILL BE KNOWN OF THE OTHER.... I BEQUEATH THE WHOLE OF MY PROPERTY ... TO THE UNITED STATES OF AMERICA TO FOUND AT WASHINGTON THE SMITHSONIAN INSTITUTION, AN ESTABLISHMENT FOR THE INCREASE AND DIFFUSION OF KNOWLEDGE AMONG MEN.

—James Smithson

OF ALL THE FOUNDATIONS OF ESTABLISHMENTS FOR PIOUS OR CHARITABLE USES WHICH EVER SIGNALIZED THE SPIRIT OF THE AGE, OR THE COMPREHENSIVE BENEFICENCE OF THE FOUNDER, NONE CAN BE NAMED MORE DESERVING OF THE APPROBATION OF MANKIND THAN THE SMITHSONIAN INSTITUTION. SHOULD IT BE FAITHFULLY CARRIED INTO EFFECT, WITH AN EARNESTNESS AND SAGACITY OF APPLICATION ... PROPORTIONED TO THE MEANS FURNISHED BY THE WILL OF THE FOUNDER, AND TO THE GREATNESS AND SIMPLICITY OF HIS DESIGN AS BY HIMSELF DECLARED, "THE INCREASE AND DIFFUSION OF KNOWLEDGE AMONG MEN," HIS NAME WILL BE HEREAFTER ENROLLED AMONG THE EMINENT BENEFACTORS OF MANKIND ... WHOEVER INCREASES KNOWLEDGE, MULTIPLIES THE USES TO WHICH HE IS ABLE TO TURN THE GIFTS OF HIS CREATOR.

—John Quincy Adams

MODERN CIVILIZATION DEPENDS ON SCIENCE.... JAMES SMITHSON WAS WELL AWARE THAT KNOWLEDGE SHOULD NOT BE VIEWED AS EXISTING IN ISOLATED PARTS, BUT AS A WHOLE, EACH PORTION OF WHICH THROWS LIGHT ON ALL THE OTHER, AND THAT THE TENDENCY OF ALL IS TO IMPROVE THE HUMAN MIND, AND GIVE IT NEW SOURCES OF POWER AND ENJOYMENT.... NARROW MINDS THINK NOTHING OF IMPORTANCE BUT THEIR OWN FAVORITE PURSUIT, BUT LIBERAL VIEWS EXCLUDE NO

BRANCH OF SCIENCE OR LITERATURE, FOR THEY ALL CONTRIBUTE TO SWEETEN, TO ADORN, AND TO EMBELLISH LIFE.... SCIENCE IS THE PURSUIT ABOVE ALL WHICH IMPRESSES US WITH THE CAPACITY OF MAN FOR INTELLECTUAL AND MORAL PROGRESS AND AWAKENS THE HUMAN INTELLECT TO ASPIRATION FOR A HIGHER CONDITION OF HUMANITY.

—Joseph Henry

CONSTITUTION HALL

$\mathcal{C}$onstitution Hall, a National Historic Landmark, is part of a block-wide building complex that serves as national headquarters to the Daughters of the
American Revolution (DAR). Memorial Centennial Hall, genealogical and historic
research libraries, period rooms, banquet and assembly rooms, a museum, an Ameri-
cana collection, and administrative offices are also part of the complex.

Completed in 1929, Constitution Hall is the work of the architect John Russell
Pope. Pope also designed the Jefferson Memorial, the National Gallery of Art building, and the National Archives building. The structure is made of Alabama limestone
and abounds with American decorative motifs.

While the building was originally constructed for DAR functions, Constitution Hall, which seats 4,000, is used for a variety of cultural and literary activities. For more than four decades, until the completion of the Kennedy Center for the Performing Arts, Constitution Hall was where the National Symphony Orchestra performed. The hall remains the site of annual DAR meetings as well as public lectures, concerts, films, graduation ceremonies, and other related programs.

Constitution Hall is located near the White House on 18th Street, between C and D Streets. The building's inscriptions are found near the bronze door entrance to the auditorium.

ℰ᷍ꜱ

LET US RAISE A STANDARD TO WHICH THE WISE AND HONEST CAN REPAIR. THE EVENT IS IN THE HANDS OF GOD.

—*George Washington*

LET OUR OBJECT BE OUR COUNTRY, OUR WHOLE COUNTRY, AND NOTHING BUT OUR COUNTRY.

—*Daniel Webster*

REMOVE NOT THE ANCIENT LANDMARK WHICH THY FATHERS HAVE SET.

—The Holy Bible, *Proverbs 22:28*

VIETNAM VETERANS MEMORIAL

*A*mong Washington's most prominent and treasured sites is the Vietnam Veterans Memorial, which honors Americans who served in the Vietnam War. The polished black granite of the memorial known as the Wall bears the names of the 58,191 Americans who gave their lives in that conflict and is designed in such a way that the names of the war dead themselves serve as their tribute.

The memorial is the work of Maya Ying Lin who, as a 21-year-old student at Yale, submitted the winning design to a national competition with more than 14,000 entries. Dedicated on November 11, 1982, the memorial is a place where the ground has been laid open, and where reflective stone embraces the earth. Established through extensive private efforts and funds, the Wall is a deeply personal monument, strewn with flowers, flags, notes, and mementos left by the scores who visit it daily.

Adjoining the memorial is a statue of three American soldiers designed by Frederick Hart. Also adjacent to the site is the Vietnam Women's Memorial, which was dedicated on

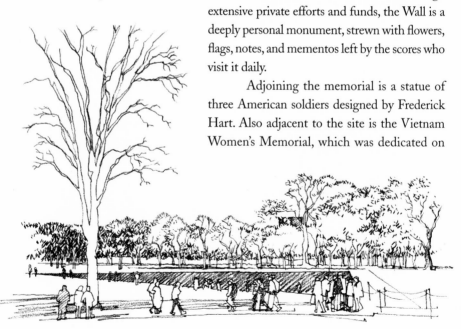

November 11, 1993. The bronze sculpture created by Glenna Goodacre commemorates the invaluable contributions of the more than 265,000 women who served in the war.

1959-1975

Panel 1E

IN HONOR OF THE MEN AND WOMEN OF THE ARMED FORCES OF THE UNITED STATES WHO SERVED IN THE VIETNAM WAR. THE NAMES OF THOSE WHO GAVE THEIR LIVES AND OF THOSE WHO REMAIN MISSING ARE INSCRIBED IN THE ORDER THEY WERE TAKEN FROM US.

Panel 1W

OUR NATION HONORS THE COURAGE, SACRIFICE AND DEVOTION TO DUTY AND COUNTRY OF ITS VIETNAM VETERANS. THIS MEMORIAL WAS BUILT WITH PRIVATE CONTRIBUTIONS FROM THE AMERICAN PEOPLE.

November 11, 1982

THIS FLAGPOLE REPRESENTS THE SERVICE RENDERED TO OUR COUNTRY BY THE VETERANS OF THE VIETNAM WAR. THE FLAG AFFIRMS THE PRINCIPLES OF FREEDOM FOR WHICH THEY FOUGHT AND THEIR PRIDE IN HAVING SERVED UNDER DIFFICULT CIRCUMSTANCES.

Flagpole inscription

LINCOLN MEMORIAL

Known for his towering height and character, Abraham Lincoln is one of the most commanding figures in American history. A self-educated man, he was shaped by the human hardships of life on the American frontier and by his deep faith in a "living God" who "has his own purposes."

Lincoln served in the Illinois legislature and in the U.S. House of Representatives. Even though he failed in candidacies for the Senate and the vice presidency in the 1850s, his views became widely known. In 1860, just prior to the Civil War, Lincoln became president, and was re-elected in 1864.

The Civil War dominated Lincoln's presidency. Devoted to preserving the Union, he actively directed war efforts, frequently overruling his commanders. In 1863, Lincoln issued the Emancipation Proclamation abolishing slavery, which later became the basis for the Thirteenth Amendment to the Constitution. Shortly after the war, on April 14, 1865, Lincoln was shot by John Wilkes Booth at Ford's Theatre in Washington, D.C. The president died the following day.

Contained within the Lincoln Memorial are the Gettysburg Address, which honored the Civil War dead, and Lincoln's Second Inaugural Address, directed at re-unifying a divided nation. Completed in 1922, the memorial was designed by Henry Bacon. The 19-foot statue of Lincoln is the work of Daniel Chester French.

❧

IN THIS TEMPLE, AS IN THE HEARTS OF THE PEOPLE
FOR WHOM HE SAVED THE UNION, THE MEMORY OF
ABRAHAM LINCOLN IS ENSHRINED FOREVER.

—Dedicatory Inscription

FOUR SCORE AND SEVEN YEARS AGO OUR FATHERS BROUGHT FORTH ON THIS CONTINENT A NEW NATION CONCEIVED IN LIBERTY AND DEDICATED TO THE PROPOSITION THAT ALL MEN ARE CREATED EQUAL.

NOW WE ARE ENGAGED IN A GREAT CIVIL WAR TESTING WHETHER THAT NATION OR ANY NATION SO CONCEIVED AND SO DEDICATED CAN LONG ENDURE. WE ARE MET ON A GREAT BATTLEFIELD OF THAT WAR. WE HAVE COME TO DEDICATE A PORTION OF THAT FIELD AS A FINAL RESTING PLACE FOR THOSE WHO HERE GAVE THEIR LIVES THAT THAT NATION MIGHT LIVE. IT IS ALTOGETHER FITTING AND PROPER THAT WE SHOULD DO THIS. BUT IN A LARGER SENSE WE CAN NOT DEDICATE—WE CAN NOT CONSECRATE—WE CAN NOT HALLOW— THIS GROUND. THE BRAVE MEN LIVING AND DEAD WHO STRUGGLED HERE HAVE CONSECRATED IT FAR ABOVE OUR POWER TO ADD OR DETRACT. THE WORLD WILL LITTLE NOTE NOR LONG REMEMBER WHAT WE SAY HERE BUT IT CAN NEVER FORGET WHAT THEY DID HERE. IT IS FOR US THE LIVING RATHER TO BE DEDICATED HERE TO THE UNFINISHED WORK WHICH THEY WHO FOUGHT HERE HAVE THUS FAR SO NOBLY ADVANCED. IT IS RATHER FOR US TO BE HERE DEDICATED TO THE GREAT TASK REMAINING BEFORE US—THAT FROM THESE HONORED DEAD WE TAKE INCREASED DEVOTION TO THAT CAUSE FOR WHICH THEY GAVE THE LAST FULL MEASURE OF DEVOTION—THAT WE HERE HIGHLY RESOLVE THAT THESE DEAD SHALL NOT HAVE DIED IN VAIN—THAT THIS

NATION UNDER GOD SHALL HAVE A NEW BIRTH OF FREEDOM—AND
THAT GOVERNMENT OF THE PEOPLE BY THE PEOPLE AND FOR THE
PEOPLE SHALL NOT PERISH FROM THE EARTH.

☙

FELLOW COUNTRYMEN:

AT THIS SECOND APPEARING TO TAKE THE OATH OF THE PRESI-
DENTIAL OFFICE THERE IS LESS OCCASION FOR AN EXTENDED ADDRESS
THAN THERE WAS AT THE FIRST.
THEN A STATEMENT SOME-
WHAT IN DETAIL OF A COURSE
TO BE PURSUED SEEMED
FITTING AND PROPER.

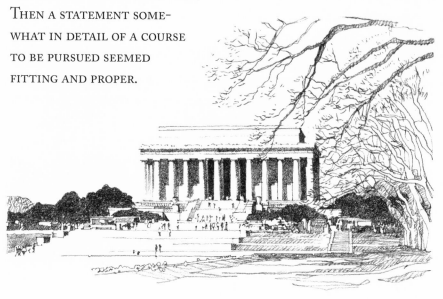

Now at the expiration of four years, during which public declarations have been constantly called forth on every point and phase of the great contest which still absorbs the attention and engrosses the energies of the nation, little that is new could be presented. The progress of our arms, upon which all else chiefly depends, is as well known to the public as to myself, and it is, I trust, reasonably satisfactory and encouraging to all. With high hope for the future, no prediction in regard to it is ventured.

On the occasion corresponding to this four years ago all thoughts were anxiously directed to an impending civil war. All dreaded it, all sought to avert it. While the inaugural address was being delivered from this place, devoted altogether to saving the Union without war, insurgent agents were in the city seeking to destroy it without war—seeking to dissolve the Union and divide effects by negotiation. Both parties deprecated war, but one of them would make war rather than let the nation survive, and the other would accept war rather than let it perish. And the war came.

One-eighth of the whole population were colored slaves, not distributed generally over the Union, but localized

IN THE SOUTHERN PART OF IT. THESE SLAVES CONSTITUTED A PECU-
LIAR AND POWERFUL INTEREST. ALL KNEW THAT THIS INTEREST WAS
THE CAUSE OF THE WAR. TO STRENGTHEN, PERPETUATE, AND EXTEND
THIS INTEREST WAS THE OBJECT FOR WHICH THE INSURGENTS WOULD
REND THE UNION EVEN BY WAR, WHILE THE GOVERNMENT CLAIMED
NO RIGHT TO DO MORE THAN TO RESTRICT THE TERRITORIAL ENLARGE-
MENT OF IT. NEITHER PARTY EXPECTED FOR THE WAR THE MAGNITUDE
OR THE DURATION WHICH IT HAS ALREADY ATTAINED. NEITHER AN-
TICIPATED THAT THE CAUSE OF THE CONFLICT MIGHT CEASE WITH OR
EVEN BEFORE THE CONFLICT ITSELF SHOULD CEASE. EACH LOOKED FOR
AN EASIER TRIUMPH AND A RESULT LESS FUNDAMENTAL AND ASTOUND-
ING. BOTH READ THE SAME BIBLE AND PRAY TO THE SAME GOD, AND
EACH INVOKES HIS AID AGAINST THE OTHER. IT MAY SEEM STRANGE
THAT ANY MEN SHOULD DARE TO ASK A JUST GOD'S ASSISTANCE IN
WRINGING THEIR BREAD FROM THE SWEAT OF OTHER MEN'S FACES, BUT
LET US JUDGE NOT, THAT WE BE NOT JUDGED. THE PRAYERS OF BOTH
COULD NOT BE ANSWERED. THAT OF NEITHER HAS BEEN ANSWERED
FULLY. THE ALMIGHTY HAS HIS OWN PURPOSES. "WOE UNTO THE
WORLD BECAUSE OF OFFENSES; FOR IT MUST NEEDS BE THAT OFFENSES
COME, BUT WOE TO THAT MAN BY WHOM THE OFFENSE COMETH."
IF WE SHALL SUPPOSE THAT AMERICAN SLAVERY IS ONE OF THOSE
OFFENSES WHICH, IN THE PROVIDENCE OF GOD MUST NEEDS COME,

BUT WHICH, HAVING CONTINUED THROUGH HIS APPOINTED TIME, HE NOW WILLS TO REMOVE, AND THAT HE GIVES TO BOTH NORTH AND SOUTH THIS TERRIBLE WAR AS THE WOE DUE TO THOSE BY WHOM THE OFFENSE CAME, SHALL WE DISCERN THEREIN ANY DEPARTURE FROM THOSE DIVINE ATTRIBUTES WHICH THE BELIEVERS IN A LIVING GOD ALWAYS ASCRIBE TO HIM. FONDLY DO WE HOPE, FERVENTLY DO WE PRAY, THAT THIS MIGHTY SCOURGE OF WAR MAY SPEEDILY PASS AWAY. YET, IF GOD WILLS THAT IT CONTINUE UNTIL ALL THE WEALTH PILED BY THE BONDSMAN'S TWO HUNDRED AND FIFTY YEARS OF UNREQUITED TOIL SHALL BE SUNK, AND UNTIL EVERY DROP OF BLOOD DRAWN WITH THE LASH SHALL BE PAID BY ANOTHER DRAWN WITH THE SWORD, AS WAS SAID THREE THOUSAND YEARS AGO, SO STILL IT MUST BE SAID "THE JUDGMENTS OF THE LORD ARE TRUE AND RIGHTEOUS ALTOGETHER."

WITH MALICE TOWARD NONE, WITH CHARITY FOR ALL, WITH FIRMNESS IN THE RIGHT AS GOD GIVES US TO SEE THE RIGHT, LET US STRIVE ON TO FINISH THE WORK WE ARE IN, TO BIND UP THE NATION'S WOUNDS, TO CARE FOR HIM WHO SHALL HAVE BORNE THE BATTLE AND FOR HIS WIDOW AND HIS ORPHAN, TO DO ALL WHICH MAY ACHIEVE AND CHERISH A JUST AND LASTING PEACE AMONG OURSELVES AND WITH ALL NATIONS.

JOHN F. KENNEDY CENTER
FOR THE PERFORMING ARTS

*T*he John F. Kennedy Center for the Performing Arts is the sole official memorial to President Kennedy. Efforts to establish such an arts center in Washington began in 1958 when President Eisenhower signed the National Cultural Center Act, but progress stalled due to lack of funds. In 1963, at a White House luncheon, President Kennedy implored the business community for the financial contributions necessary to complete the project. Shortly after Kennedy's death, when an offer was made to have the center serve as a permanent memorial to the president, the Kennedy family accepted the proposal. A ground-breaking ceremony was held in 1964. Designed by Edward Durrell Stone and completed in 1971, the building is sited on the Potomac River, east of Theodore Roosevelt Island.

Intended as a "place for the human spirit," the center is adorned with gifts from more than 40 countries and contains multiple theaters with a combined seating capacity exceeding 6,500. It is home to the Washington Opera and the National

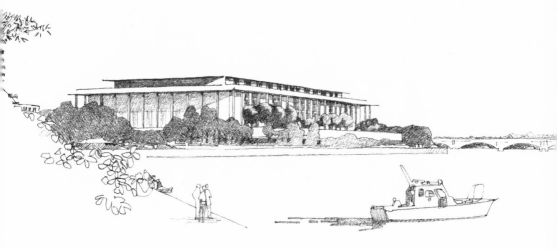

Symphony Orchestra. The 630-foot long Grand Foyer contains a 7-foot bronze bust of President Kennedy by Robert Berks. Inscriptions from Kennedy's writings and speeches are found on the exterior wall of the building's west terrace.

❧

I LOOK FORWARD TO AN AMERICA WHICH WILL REWARD ACHIEVEMENT IN THE ARTS AS WE REWARD ACHIEVEMENT IN BUSINESS OR STATECRAFT. I LOOK FORWARD TO AN AMERICA WHICH WILL STEADILY RAISE THE STANDARDS OF ARTISTIC ACCOMPLISHMENT AND WHICH WILL STEADILY ENLARGE CULTURAL OPPORTUNITIES FOR ALL OF OUR CITIZENS. AND I LOOK FORWARD TO AN AMERICA WHICH COMMANDS RESPECT THROUGHOUT THE WORLD NOT ONLY FOR ITS STRENGTH BUT FOR ITS CIVILIZATION AS WELL.

THIS COUNTRY CANNOT AFFORD TO BE MATERIALLY RICH
AND SPIRITUALLY POOR.

TO FURTHER THE APPRECIATION OF CULTURE AMONG ALL THE
PEOPLE, TO INCREASE RESPECT FOR THE CREATIVE INDIVIDUAL,
TO WIDEN PARTICIPATION BY ALL THE PROCESSES AND
FULFILLMENTS OF ART—THIS IS ONE OF THE FASCINATING
CHALLENGES OF THESE DAYS.

THERE IS A CONNECTION, HARD TO EXPLAIN LOGICALLY BUT EASY TO FEEL, BETWEEN ACHIEVEMENT IN PUBLIC LIFE AND PROGRESS IN THE ARTS. THE AGE OF PERICLES WAS ALSO THE AGE OF PHIDIAS. THE AGE OF LORENZO DE MEDICI WAS ALSO THE AGE OF LEONARDO DA VINCI. THE AGE OF ELIZABETH WAS ALSO THE AGE OF SHAKESPEARE. AND THE NEW FRONTIER FOR WHICH I CAMPAIGN IN PUBLIC LIFE, CAN ALSO BE A NEW FRONTIER FOR AMERICAN ART.

I LOOK FORWARD TO AN AMERICA WHICH WILL NOT
BE AFRAID OF GRACE AND BEAUTY.

I AM CERTAIN THAT AFTER THE DUST OF CENTURIES HAS PASSED
OVER OUR CITIES, WE, TOO, WILL BE REMEMBERED NOT FOR VICTORIES
OR DEFEATS IN BATTLE OR POLITICS, BUT FOR OUR CONTRIBUTION
TO THE HUMAN SPIRIT.

THEODORE ROOSEVELT MEMORIAL

*T*heodore Roosevelt was as at home in the Dakota Territory as in the White House, as widely known for his bravery as a "Rough Rider" in the Spanish-American War as he was for the mediation of a treaty between Russia and Japan for which he received the Nobel Peace Prize in 1906.

Born in 1858, Roosevelt married Alice Hathaway Lee in 1880. She died four years later in childbirth, and he subsequently married Edith Kermit Carow. After attending Harvard, Roosevelt entered politics and held state and national offices, including that of vice president under William McKinley. When McKinley was assassinated in 1901, Roosevelt became president. He was elected to a full presidential term in 1905. However, he was unsuccessful in his 1912 presidential attempt as a "Bull Moose" candidate.

A naturalist and conservationist, Roosevelt was instrumental in establishing five national parks and in setting aside 234 million acres of land for public use and protection. He died in Long Island, New York, in 1919.

In 1932, an 88-acre island in the Potomac River between the Memorial and Key bridges was purchased as a wildlife refuge and preserve in his memory. At the island's center is a memorial consisting of fountains, walls inscribed with excerpts from Roosevelt's writings and speeches, and a 17-foot bronze statue of Roosevelt by Paul Manship. The memorial was designed by Eric Gugler.

THE STATE

OURS IS A DEMOCRACY OF LIBERTY BY, THROUGH,
AND UNDER THE LAW.

A GREAT DEMOCRACY HAS GOT TO BE PROGRESSIVE OR IT WILL SOON
CEASE TO BE GREAT OR A DEMOCRACY.

ORDER WITHOUT LIBERTY AND LIBERTY WITHOUT ORDER ARE
EQUALLY DESTRUCTIVE.

IN POPULAR GOVERNMENT RESULTS WORTH HAVING CAN BE
ACHIEVED ONLY BY MEN WHO CAN COMBINE WORTHY IDEALS
WITH PRACTICAL GOOD SENSE.

IF I MUST CHOOSE BETWEEN RIGHTEOUSNESS AND PEACE I CHOOSE
RIGHTEOUSNESS.

YOUTH

I WANT TO SEE YOU GAME, BOYS, I WANT TO SEE YOU BRAVE AND
MANLY, AND I ALSO WANT TO SEE YOU GENTLE AND TENDER.

BE PRACTICAL AS WELL AS GENEROUS IN YOUR IDEALS.
KEEP YOUR EYES ON THE STARS, BUT REMEMBER TO KEEP
YOUR FEET ON THE GROUND.

COURAGE, HARD WORK, SELF-MASTERY, AND INTELLIGENT EFFORT
ARE ALL ESSENTIAL TO SUCCESSFUL LIFE.

ALIKE FOR THE NATION AND THE INDIVIDUAL, THE ONE
INDISPENSABLE REQUISITE IS CHARACTER.

MANHOOD

A MAN'S USEFULNESS DEPENDS UPON HIS LIVING UP TO
HIS IDEALS IN SO FAR AS HE CAN.

IT IS HARD TO FAIL, BUT IT IS WORSE NEVER TO
HAVE TRIED TO SUCCEED.

ALL DARING AND COURAGE, ALL IRON ENDURANCE OF MISFORTUNE
MAKE FOR A FINER AND NOBLER TYPE OF MANHOOD.

ONLY THOSE ARE FIT TO LIVE WHO DO NOT FEAR TO DIE;
AND NONE ARE FIT TO DIE WHO HAVE SHRUNK FROM THE
JOY OF LIFE AND THE DUTY OF LIFE.

NATURE
THERE IS DELIGHT IN THE HARDY LIFE OF THE OPEN.

THERE ARE NO WORDS THAT CAN TELL THE HIDDEN SPIRIT OF
THE WILDERNESS, THAT CAN REVEAL ITS MYSTERY, ITS MELANCHOLY,
AND ITS CHARM.

THE NATION BEHAVES WELL IF IT TREATS THE NATURAL RESOURCES
AS ASSETS WHICH IT MUST TURN OVER TO THE NEXT GENERATION
INCREASED, AND NOT IMPAIRED, IN VALUE.

CONSERVATION MEANS DEVELOPMENT AS MUCH AS
IT DOES PROTECTION.

ARLINGTON NATIONAL CEMETERY

rlington National Cemetery is the best known of the 85 national cemeteries found throughout the United States. Established on property that belonged to the family of Robert E. Lee and originally intended as a burial ground for the Union dead, it is the site of the graves of Presidents John F. Kennedy and William Taft and scores of other Americans who served their country in the military.

It is also the site of the Tomb of the Unknowns, which commemorates the lives of the thousands of American soldiers whose bodies could not be retrieved or identified. Interred in it are the remains of four unknown servicemen from World Wars I and II and the Korean and Vietnam wars. It is guarded day and night by members of the Army's Third United States Infantry. The marble tomb was designed by the sculptor Thomas Hudson Jones and by the architect Lorimer Rich.

Adjoining the Tomb of the Unknowns is the Arlington Memorial Amphitheater, designed by Carrere and Hastings of New York as a place to hold commemorative services for the honored war dead. President Woodrow Wilson laid the cornerstone for the white Vermont marble structure in 1915, and construction was completed in 1920. Inscriptions are found above the stage.

Tomb of the Unknowns

HERE RESTS IN HONORED GLORY AN AMERICAN SOLDIER
KNOWN BUT TO GOD.

Arlington Memorial Amphitheater

DULCE ET DECORUM EST PRO PATRIA MORI.
(IT IS SWEET AND FITTING TO DIE FOR ONE'S COUNTRY.)

WE HERE HIGHLY RESOLVE THAT THESE DEAD
SHALL NOT HAVE DIED IN VAIN.

—Abraham Lincoln

WHEN WE ASSUMED THE SOLDIER, WE DID NOT
LAY ASIDE THE CITIZEN.

—George Washington

JOHN F. KENNEDY AND ROBERT F. KENNEDY GRAVESITES

*A*mong the most visited graves at Arlington National Cemetery are those of John F. Kennedy and Robert F. Kennedy. Born in 1917, John F. Kennedy was educated at Harvard and became a noted writer. A decorated war hero, Kennedy served in Congress shortly after his military service. He was elected to the presidency in 1960, and Cold War tensions dominated his term in office. However, his administration also established the Peace Corps, committed the United States to outer space exploration, and made considerable progress in the area of civil rights. Kennedy was killed by an assassin on November 22, 1963, in Dallas, Texas.

An eternal flame marks his grave. Buried beside him are his wife, Jacqueline Kennedy Onassis, their son Patrick, who died as an infant, and their unnamed still-born daughter.

Robert F. Kennedy was born in 1925. When he was 35, he was appointed United States attorney general by his brother, President Kennedy. Following the president's assassination, Kennedy was elected to the U. S. Senate. Disagreement with President Lyndon B. Johnson over the Vietnam War caused him to run for the executive office. After winning the California Democratic presidential primary, Kennedy was shot at the Ambassador Hotel in Los Angeles. He died hours later on June 6, 1968. His grave is marked by a small white wooden cross.

John F. Kennedy Gravesite

The inscriptions are from Kennedy's inaugural address.

John Fitzgerald Kennedy

1917-1963

LET THE WORD GO FORTH FROM THIS TIME AND PLACE, TO FRIEND AND FOE ALIKE, THAT THE TORCH HAS BEEN PASSED TO A NEW GENERATION OF AMERICANS.

LET EVERY NATION KNOW, WHETHER IT WISHES US WELL OR ILL, THAT WE SHALL PAY ANY PRICE, BEAR ANY BURDEN, MEET ANY HARDSHIP, SUPPORT ANY FRIEND, OPPOSE ANY FOE TO ASSURE THE SURVIVAL AND THE SUCCESS OF LIBERTY.

NOW THE TRUMPET SUMMONS US AGAIN—NOT AS A CALL TO BEAR ARMS, THOUGH ARMS WE NEED—NOT AS A CALL TO BATTLE, THOUGH EMBATTLED WE ARE—BUT A CALL TO BEAR THE BURDEN OF A LONG TWILIGHT STRUGGLE—A STRUGGLE AGAINST THE COMMON ENEMIES OF MAN: TYRANNY, POVERTY, DISEASE, AND WAR ITSELF.

IN THE LONG HISTORY OF THE WORLD, ONLY A FEW GENERATIONS HAVE BEEN GRANTED THE ROLE OF DEFENDING FREEDOM IN ITS HOUR OF MAXIMUM DANGER. I DO NOT SHRINK FROM THIS RESPONSIBILITY— I WELCOME IT.

THE ENERGY, THE FAITH, THE DEVOTION WHICH WE BRING TO THIS ENDEAVOR WILL LIGHT OUR COUNTRY AND ALL WHO SERVE IT— AND THE GLOW FROM THAT FIRE CAN TRULY LIGHT THE WORLD.

AND SO, MY FELLOW AMERICANS: ASK NOT WHAT YOUR COUNTRY CAN DO FOR YOU—ASK WHAT YOU CAN DO FOR YOUR COUNTRY. MY FELLOW CITIZENS OF THE WORLD: ASK NOT WHAT AMERICA WILL DO FOR YOU, BUT WHAT TOGETHER WE CAN DO FOR THE FREEDOM OF MAN.

WITH A GOOD CONSCIENCE OUR ONLY SURE REWARD, WITH HISTORY THE FINAL JUDGE OF OUR DEEDS, LET US GO FORTH TO LEAD THE LAND WE LOVE, ASKING HIS BLESSING AND HIS HELP, BUT KNOWING THAT HERE ON EARTH GOD'S WORK MUST TRULY BE OUR OWN.

Robert F. Kennedy Gravesite

The first inscription is from Kennedy's "Day of Affirmation" address given at the University of Capetown, South Africa, in 1966; the second is from his 1968 eulogy for Dr. Martin Luther King, Jr.

ROBERT FRANCIS KENNEDY
1925-1968

IT IS FROM NUMBERLESS DIVERSE ACTS OF COURAGE AND BELIEF THAT HUMAN HISTORY IS SHAPED. EACH TIME A MAN STANDS UP FOR AN IDEAL, OR ACTS TO IMPROVE THE LOT OF OTHERS, OR STRIKES OUT AGAINST INJUSTICE, HE SENDS FORTH A TINY RIPPLE OF HOPE, AND

CROSSING EACH OTHER FROM A MILLION DIFFERENT CENTERS OF ENERGY AND DARING THOSE RIPPLES BUILD A CURRENT WHICH CAN SWEEP DOWN THE MIGHTIEST WALLS OF OPPRESSION AND RESISTANCE.

౭ఎ

AESCHYLUS WROTE: "IN OUR SLEEP, PAIN THAT CANNOT FORGET FALLS DROP BY DROP UPON THE HEART AND IN OUR DESPAIR, AGAINST OUR WILL, COMES WISDOM THROUGH THE AWFUL GRACE OF GOD."

WHAT WE NEED IN THE UNITED STATES IS NOT DIVISION. WHAT WE NEED IN THE UNITED STATES IS NOT HATRED. WHAT WE NEED IN THE UNITED STATES IS NOT VIOLENCE OR LAWLESSNESS, BUT LOVE AND WISDOM AND COMPASSION TOWARD ONE ANOTHER, AND A FEELING OF JUSTICE TOWARD THOSE WHO STILL SUFFER WITHIN OUR COUNTRY WHETHER THEY BE WHITE OR THEY BE BLACK. LET US DEDI-CATE OURSELVES TO WHAT THE GREEKS WROTE SO MANY YEARS AGO: TO TAME THE SAVAGENESS OF MAN AND MAKE GENTLE THE LIFE OF THIS WORLD. LET US DEDICATE OURSELVES TO THAT AND SAY A PRAYER FOR OUR COUNTRY AND OUR PEOPLE.

INDEX

1 JEFFERSON MEMORIAL
14th Street and E. Basin
Drive, SW

2 UNITED STATES HOLOCAUST
MEMORIAL MUSEUM
100 Raoul Wallenberg Place
(between D Street and
Independence Avenue, SW)

3 DEPARTMENT OF AGRICULTURE
14th Street and Independence
Avenue, SW

LIBRARY OF CONGRESS:

4 THOMAS JEFFERSON BUILDING
1st Street and Independence
Avenue, SE

5 JOHN ADAMS BUILDING
2nd Street and Independence
Avenue, SE

6 JAMES MADISON MEMORIAL
BUILDING
101 Independence Avenue, SE

7 FOLGER SHAKESPEARE LIBRARY
201 E. Capitol Street, SE

8 MARY McLEOD BETHUNE
MEMORIAL
Lincoln Park, E. Capitol and
12th Streets, NE

9 SUPREME COURT OF THE
UNITED STATES
1st Street, NE (between Maryland
Avenue and E. Capitol Street)

10 UNITED STATES CAPITOL
Entrance at E. Capitol Street on
Capitol Hill

11 ROBERT A. TAFT MEMORIAL
Capitol Grounds (between
Constitution, New Jersey, and
Louisiana Avenues, NW)

12 UNION STATION
Massachusetts Avenue, NE
(between 1st and 2nd Streets)

13 NATIONAL POSTAL MUSEUM
Massachusetts Avenue, NE
(between N. Capitol and 1st
Streets)

14 NATIONAL ARCHIVES
Constitution Avenue and 8th
Street, NW

15 DEPARTMENT OF JUSTICE
9th Street and Constitution
Avenue, NW

16 FORMER POST OFFICE
DEPARTMENT BUILDING
12th Street and Pennsylvania
Avenue, NW

17 FREEDOM PLAZA
Pennsylvania Avenue, NW
(between 13th and 14th Streets)

18 DEPARTMENT OF COMMERCE
14th Street, NW (between E
Street and Constitution Avenue)

19 NATIONAL MUSEUM
OF AMERICAN HISTORY
Constitution Avenue and 14th
Street, NW

20 CONSTITUTION HALL
18th and D Streets, NW

21 VIETNAM VETERANS MEMORIAL
21st Street and Constitution
Avenue, NW

22 LINCOLN MEMORIAL
23rd Street, NW (west end of
Mall)

23 JOHN F. KENNEDY CENTER
FOR THE PERFORMING ARTS
New Hampshire Avenue, NW,
and Rock Creek Parkway

24 THEODORE ROOSEVELT
MEMORIAL
Roosevelt Island, Potomac River
(adjacent to the George
Washington Memorial Parkway
and Key Bridge)

ARLINGTON NATIONAL
CEMETERY:

25 TOMB OF THE UNKNOWNS
off Memorial Drive

26 ARLINGTON MEMORIAL
AMPHITHEATER
off Memorial Drive

27 JOHN F. KENNEDY AND ROBERT
F. KENNEDY GRAVESITES
off Sheridan Drive, Arlington
National Cemetery